This book is being given to:

_____

because I care and support you on your journey.

_____

PRAISE FOR DR. TIM BENSON AND SURVIVING SUCCESS

Dr. Tim Benson has always had what I call — "IT." When he played football for me at Hampton University, he had — "IT." As a student in the classroom, he always had – "IT." As an author, father, husband, a leader in his chosen field — he has — "IT." As a college coach for over 40 years, I have been blessed to meet thousands of outstanding people — adminis- trators, coaches and players. Coaches are constantly evaluating talent and describing that talent with ease. Once in a while, we become speechless trying to explain overwhelming talent. At that point we simply say — He has — "IT." Dr. Tim Benson is an awesome talent and his book – "Surviving Success" – is a must-read book. This book meets you where you are and gives you a guide for sustainability moving forward. This book has — "IT."
— *Joe Taylor,*
College football coach (233-96-4), Mentor, Motivational Speaker
Author of The Making of a Champion"

"We are never taught one of the most important skills needed for all areas of our lives; how to Survive Success! If you're an achiever who is experiencing any level of success, then read and absorb the strategies in this brilliant book by my friend Dr. Tim Benson! This could be one of the most important books you will ever read!"
— *James Malinchak*
Featured on ABCs Hit TV Show,"Secret Millionaire"
Author of the Top-Selling Book, Millionaire Success Secrets
Founder, www.BigMoneySpeaker.com

"One of the things that I like to tell our guys is that when they know better, they do better in terms of dealing with money and

other things associated with becoming a professional athlete. I also tell them that talent will get them here on the professional level but it won't keep them here. There are plenty of good athletes that made it but were not successful because they were lacking in other areas that had nothing to do with their skill level. The concepts taught in this book not only initiate a much needed dialog but also lower the threshold for getting help."
— *Maurice Kelly*
Senior Director of Player Engagement
Seattle Seahawks

"I've known Dr. Tim Benson for over 10 years. We worked side-by-side in the aftermaths of Hurricane Katrina and the earthquake in Haiti. I know his core values. In the same way he has aided victims of natural disasters he uses his knowledge and clinical expertise to help those who've experienced personal disasters brought on by instant success. This wise book is his gift to us."
— *Bruce H. Price, M.D.*
Associate Professor of Neurology,
Harvard Medical School

The brilliance of this book is the depth of research and knowledge Dr. Benson shares. It goes way past surface level, and into what it really takes to thrive as an executive, scholar, or athlete. This book isn't just inspiring, but very tactical and comprehensive. It walks you through step by step how to survive the pinnacles of success, and how to deal with rock bottoms. This book should be required for everybody entering school, athletics, or business. I assure you this book will change the game for you.
— *Peter Voogd,*
Leading Authority for Young Entrepreneurs,
CEO of GameChangersMovement.com

"Enduring one's own success is to understand "thy self"-first. When you are achieving and succeeding by all accounts the accolades, honors, power are extremely intoxicating. We can reach a point in our careers when success feels meaningless, therefore, making it difficult to conceive of failure until its right around the corner. Only then, is when you realize your failure is about to happen because of unaddressed weaknesses and vanity. This book is the key to helping you stay focused on who and what you are as you continue to strive towards your best self."
— *Mark A.Conrad*
Director of The Bridge Program,
Bridgewater State University

"Having been an executive in a top fortune 500 company, I have had the privilege to be instructed by some of the best executive training coaches in the country. So I was astounded to find that Dr. Benson's words offered refreshing insight and remarkable wisdom on how to manage success. His medical background gives him the edge of empowering your psyche with self affirming guidance that can be used over and over again. Read his book once, and you begin to unlock the potential of how to stay at the top of your field. Read it over and over, and you will find deeper meaning and hidden pearls of wisdom from a man whom is living in his power and giving the world words that define his life's purpose."
— *Darryl Jones,*
VP of Sales, Marketing and Technical Services
Implant Sciences Corporation

SURVIVING SUCCESS

7 Critical Skills Needed To Thrive Under The Pressures of
The Athletic, Academic, and Professional Spotlight

Timothy G. Benson, MD

Merrimack Media

Cambridge, Massachusetts

Dedicated to Malinda Bridges Benson
and Alvin Keith Benson

CONTENTS

ACKNOWLEDGEMENTS

A project like this is not done in isolation. I want to take the time to thank many of the people who have supported me along the journey of making this book possible. I want to thank first and foremost my wife, Milca Benson and my sons, Jayden and Jordan. My brothers and sisters: Malcolm, Ivan, Martin, Bernadette and Maya. My extended family who contributed support through advice and participation in my coaching and trainings: Harold and Debra Funderburk, Roman and Milagros Matos, Cynthia and Jose Medina, Priscilla and Charles Chessher. I also want to thank all of my aunts, uncles, and cousins who have supported me throughout the years.

For those mentors who gave me opportunities and encouragement when I needed it the most, I want to thank: Dean Brenda Lee, Allen Counter, Bruce Price, Roger Weiss, Shelly Greenfield, Joan Reede, Alvin Poussaint, William and Norma Harvey, Pastors Ray and Gloria Hammond, Teresa Spillane, Edward Messner and Anne Alonso.

I would like to thank both my athletic and professional coaches for helping to bring out my best: Pete Adkins, Joe Taylor, James Malinchak, Brendon Burchard, Jonathan Sprinkles and Bo Eason.

To those who helped me get this book across the finish line,

I want to thank: Stuart Horwitz, Doug Childress, and Jenny Hudson.

There are countless number of friends and colleagues who not only supported me on this journey, but more important, helped me stay on track. Although there are too many to mention, I want to specifically acknowledge: Darryl Jones, Nicole Roberts Jones, Mark Conrad, Jacqui Conrad, Marla Frederick, Sue Rees, Sarah Benton, Hilary Connery, Nancy Merrill, Steve Brannon, Frank Verdugo, Alan Brown, Chaundre Cross, and my brothers of the Gamma Iota and Epsilon Gamma Lambda chapters of Alpha Phi Alpha Fraternity.

I also want to thank all of my church members, teachers and friends of Jefferson City, Missouri for helping to shape the person I am today.

PREFACE

"Tim . . . Are you there? I need an answer," the
dean on the phone asked. "Are you dropping out
or coming back to medical school?"

It had all been too much too fast. As I sat silently on the
phone, I began to reflect on my whirlwind journey toward
achieving my ultimate dream of getting into medical school.
I had done all the right things and made all the right moves. I
had earned a full football scholarship and did well in class. By
the time I graduated college I was a nationally lauded scholar
athlete, had won the Hampton University's most prestigious
honor, the president's cup. To top it all off, I gained acceptance into the University of Rochester School of Medicine
with a Dean's Scholarship. It was as if I were a first-round
draft choice. I was on top of the world! It had taken me
twenty-two years of hard work and sacrifice to achieve that
dream, and in less than two years that same dream was on the
verge of a complete disaster. Everything around me seemed
as if it were falling apart. Now I was back home on an
extended leave of absence, facing a decision that would affect
the rest of my life.

As the silence lingered, it suddenly hit me what had gone
wrong. All this time I had been learning the steps involved
for winning the prize, but no one had ever told me how to
handle it once it was attained. I was so focused on what I'd
gain, it never crossed my mind on what I would lose and

how it would affect me. No one warned me about the identity crisis that would occur with the absence of football in my life. No one told me about the dangers of having too much free time. I was never taught that I would have to learn how to deal with being average because now the whole class was comprised of 1 percenters—those individuals who were accustomed to excelling at every level. No one prepared me for how to cope with no longer being perceived as special. Who was to tell me that I would have to deal with the escalated pressure of competition while fighting off feelings of doubt and isolation? I had realized that it didn't matter how smart or talented I was, there were a whole new set of factors that would now determine my success. The game had drastically changed and I hadn't. I felt as if I were caught in the midst of a success-induced emotional storm—a silent tsunami. And I was drowning fast.

If you think a fall from grace only happens to celebrities, think again. For every Williams, Whitney, or Winehouse there are countless numbers of individuals who are secretly struggling with

> The game had drastically changed and I hadn't.

handling the unique challenges of success. Whether you are a doctor, civic leader, executive, or a professional athlete, high achievement brings universal changes to your life. Unfortunately, society prepares us very little for the challenges at this end of the spectrum, so we stumble in the darkness trying to find a way out or through.

For more than a decade as an instructor in psychiatry at Harvard Medical School, I have searched for light in the shadows of success. Numerous high performers have confided in me from my office therapy couch: Ivy League students, professional athletes, rock stars, Fortune 500 CEOs, professors, ministers, and entrepreneurs all privately sought refuge from the storm. Despite their differences they all had two things in common: a desire to get better in all senses of the word, and a need to have a safe place to exhale, to let down their guard and talk about what was really going on with them behind the mask.

Before going further, a clarification is warranted. We all define success differently. For some people it is about money, assets, experiences, or relationships. These are all significant and worthwhile. But for the purposes of this book I am defining success as a significant achievement that places you into the spotlight, therefore increasing your level of visibility and responsibility—as well as your vulnerability. You can see how, with this definition, the spotlight is not limited to celebrities and executives. It applies just as well to anyone who has achieved a major milestone that makes one standout among peers, family, or community. Success may apply to people who are the first in their families to go to college or earn graduate degrees. It can apply to entrepreneurs who have suddenly turned the corner and are getting inundated with new business. It can apply to athletes and coaches who have won championships and now have to defend their title. The list goes on and on.

Our inexperienced perception of success can be compared to the act of climbing a mountain. Step by step you climb until one day you reach the peak. Satisfied with your accomplishment, the plan is to set up camp and enjoy the view. In reality, though, most accomplishments aren't like this. Upon arriving at the peak of the mountain what you see are several other peaks that require continued climbing. The higher we climb along levels of success, the more intense the demands, pressures, and responsibilities. Unless you are prepared to handle these challenges, you may develop dysfunctional ways of handling the triumphs you have achieved so far. And who wants to take missteps and eventually fall down the mountain that took you so much energy to climb in the first place?

More often than not, when you have attained a new level, you experience the plight of the pioneer. You are forging ahead, and what is around the next corner is unclear. There is no one to guide you because the people you have relied on in the past are unfamiliar with your current challenges. You then get the sense that you are just making it up as you go. A feeling of isolation sets in. Who can really understand what you are going through? In your mind it truly becomes lonely at the top.

> Upon arriving at the peak of the mountain what you see are several other peaks that require continued climbing.

I call this point of the path "New Levels, New Devils." A more constructive path requires skills to make wise decisions. When it comes to managing success, the best practices encompass many specific skills. These range from self-acceptance to setting priorities to adopting a growth mindset. These critical skills can provide the tools to counter a series of stressors and to manage high levels of achievement effectively. Attaining success is not enough to guarantee you will retain success. Maintaining high achievement requires a completely new set of abilities and insights that are rarely discussed.

In a world focused on glamour and fame, finding clarity about what success actually means is almost as difficult as attaining success in the first place. The purpose of this book is to shed some light ahead of time on the conflicts that inevitably arise as you achieve a major accomplishment. We will talk about how to deal with your internal dialogue, as well as the external pressures associated with the spotlight. By gaining a more realistic picture of the benefits and costs of high achievement, you can not only rid yourself of illusions but also avoid the pitfalls so many experience after they reach the top.

The skills that I refer to in this book are based on the most common topics and suggestions I have used with high achievers throughout my years of practice. I write this book not as an academic exercise to prove or disprove theories. Instead, my intent is two fold: to give voice to a topic that may be too difficult or taboo to discuss, and to offer a basic guide to help navigate the treacherous psychological territory of high achievement. Let's get started.

> In a world focused on glamour and fame, finding clarity about what success actually means is almost as difficult as attaining success in the first place.

After the extended moment of silence, I answered the medical school dean on the phone. "Yes . . . I will return. I'm not quite sure yet how to handle it all, but I promised my mom that I would finish what I started. So holding on to her belief, I'm going to give it one more try."
                                                –TIMOTHY G. BENSON, MD

INTRODUCTION

NEW LEVELS, NEW DEVILS: WHY WHAT GOT YOU HERE, WON'T KEEP YOU HERE

Congratulations . . . you made it! You have achieved that long-awaited goal you have worked years for. Now you can sit back and relax, right? After all, this is what the journey was about: freedom, fame, or fortune. In essence, the good life, right?

Unfortunately, the reality is far from this fantasy we create. Major achievements always bring an array of challenges that forces us to make critical decisions about how we manage our new status in life. Being unaware of these difficulties can be a recipe for disaster, as many high achievers have realized. Before we discuss how to avoid the many pitfalls success can bring, we first have to appreciate the different types of stress associated with the spotlight. Great awareness, as well as anticipation of these challenges, is important in recognizing them, and understanding the central conflict of each allows us to make informed decisions about how to manage them. With a solid foreknowledge of these pressures we can be better equipped to react and respond to each of them as they show up in our lives.

BEING A TARGET

As you achieve higher levels of accomplishment, an increas-

ing degree of publicity is often awarded to those achievements. The more notable your success, the more attention
you draw from others. Why does this occur? Why can't you
simply become successful quietly and enjoy the benefits of
achievement without such public focus? Several reasons
account for this increase in attention, and the new spotlight
becomes a significant source of pressure because 1.) you are
more visible to others, 2.) others may view you as the yardstick for what they want to accomplish, and 3.) others may
view you as the obstacle to what they want to accomplish.

You are more visible. You are no longer the underdog that
catches people by surprise. They see you coming a mile away.
Life is a competition—a rat race. Not everyone can be the
best or attain a level of success that labels them as one of the
elite (at least by society's standards). Therefore, when individuals achieve great accomplishments, people notice. Others may notice out of admiration at first, yet, at the same time,
comparing themselves to the one who attained the accomplishment provides a source of personal assessment. For the
successful businessperson, the public wants to understand
what key ingredient allowed them to reach their lofty position. For the gifted athlete, people want to understand what
type of training and dedication was required to become a
champion. In each case, people are seeking answers that will
allow them to be more successful in their own lives. Trying to
understand a person's success as a means to incorporate positive values and habits into one's own life is a healthy exercise. But often the analysis of successful individuals moves in
another direction. If an athlete is gifted, they are suspected of
taking steroids. If a businessperson is high-achieving, she or
he is suspected of making unethical decisions on the rise to
the top. Such deceitful actions are possible of course, but it
is the unsubstantiated criticisms that I want to look at right
now. These criticisms serve to not only explain how these

specific individuals wrongfully attained high levels of achievement, but they also provide an excuse as to why others have not. People thus justify their lack of success by criticizing high-achieving individuals. They raise their own perception of themselves by reducing their opinion of others.

You become the yardstick by which everyone now measures themselves. One of the key things to remember here is that every time you move forward in life those around you are unconsciously forced to justify why they haven't. It is human nature to compare our plight to others.

> Every time you move forward in life those around you are unconsciously forced to justify why they haven't.

Instead of a critical self-analysis, it becomes easier to project one's lack of progress onto someone who is successful. The bottom line is that success brings about public recognition, and recognition can lead to inspiration or envy. With every step forward, high achievers become increasingly visible targets. What follows then is that you become the new standard by which others measure future achievements. And this not only applies to other people pursuing aspirations similar to your, it also applies to your future achievements, which will now be judged based on your past accomplishments. With every new and greater accomplishment, the bar by which the public judges you has been raised. And at some point it begins to feel that the only direction we can possibly travel is downward.

You become the obstacle. In the eyes of competitors you are not a person with feelings, you are the owner of the prize. Therefore, the focus is not on you but rather on what you have. In essence, you are in the way. As a result, it is easier for people to criticize you and insult you. Being a public target s our desire for praise against our desire to avoid criticism. We all crave praise to some degree. But to what extent? A good question to ask yourself is "how intense is my need for praise?" Seeking positive attention and praise is perfectly fine as long as you understand the transitory role it serves in life; it is "nice to have," in other words, but it cannot be a necessity. For if it is, you will be unprepared to receive criticisms. Instead, those negative appraisals can tap right into that place deep inside that holds your doubts and insecurities. I have had multiple clients who struggled with criticism because they were reminded of childhood memories when they heard either parents or other influential people tell them that they were not good enough or that they would amount to nothing. Despite working hard to disprove those predictions, no matter how successful they became, every negative remark would bring them back to those early words of discouragement.

Every time you choose to put your "stuff" out there, you are exposed to praise as well as criticism. But remember, criticizing is always easier than creating. Finding the negatives amid the positives takes much less effort than contributing new benefits to life. In fact, there will be those who use criticism as a means to gain recognition from the public themselves. Such parasitic behaviors are common and further expose high achievers to increasing levels of critique as they progress. When we internalize derogatory remarks about our accomplishments, it can be perceived as an attack on our personal character. The key is to accept that success lends you to becoming a target for such public evaluation, and both praise and criticisms will follow. Understanding your own motivations and being prepared for being in the public eye is essential to tackling this common stress of success.

COMPETING RESPONSIBILITIES

A commonly held belief contends that successful individuals have all of their priorities and responsibilities in perfect harmony and balance. We believe high achievers are so well organized they are able to juggle numerous responsibilities, all the while equally meeting every demand to great levels of satisfaction. But in reality, nothing could be further from the truth. Complete balance never exists, especially not for highly successful people, and, in fact, a degree of imbalance must exist most of the time in order to attain great accomplishments. Medical residents aren't balanced during their internships. Athletes aren't balanced in training camp or during the season. Accountants aren't balanced during tax season. In every profession there will be periods where balance is almost impossible to achieve while one strives for excellence.

Success indeed demands sacrifices. On some occasions, family responsibilities may have to be surrendered in order to meet the demands of a career or a specific pursuit. Success rarely comes easily, and in order to reach high levels of achievement, you must tolerate periods of imbalance in your life and also be willing to handle the disappointments that come with it.

The fear of disappointing others can be a real source of anxiety. As you become more successful, increasing demands are placed upon you from multiple sources. Family members and relatives continue to expect certain behaviors from you while also adding new demands related to your enhanced position in life. The public may also begin to increase their requests of you. And maintaining success has its own set of requirements. Meeting one set of demands means foregoing others, and inevitably this will result in someone being disappointed in your decisions. If we internalize this disappointment to a significant degree, it can take away from our sense of success-related fulfillment.

Being able to handle competing responsibilities means you must establish priorities, and priorities are constantly changing. Establishing such priorities proactively instead of reacting to disappointments from others allows you to maintain a healthy perspective. Likewise, developing a means by which progress can be measured enables you to justify certain sacrifices. For example, investing more time into a career goal at the expense of family time might be gauged by not only the actual accomplishment but by the secondary benefits it might bring to the family. The more you can measure your sacrifices, the less anxious you will be when disappointments inevitably arise.

High-achieving people will admit that life is rarely in a state of balance—that idea is an illusion of success that permeates society. In reality, sacrifices must be made, and imbalance must be tolerated and managed through establishing priorities. By accepting and understanding this stress as a normal part of success, you can deal more effectively with competing responsibilities from a rational perspective. Having thought things through in this manner, you can be more open and candid with others about why you made the decisions you did. They may not like the decisions you have made, but they will understand that there was care put into making them.

GREAT EXPECTATIONS

Like responsibilities, expectations change as progressive levels of success are attained. With our higher achievements, fans, friends, peers, family members, and the public at large begin to change what they expect from us. This often creates dilemmas for us in regard to deciding how we should ac. and behave. While most of us want to meet expectations, at the same time we must ensure we meet our own needs. High achievers must understand the risks involved when the expectations of others are not met. When a celebrity avoids the public, declines interviews, and creates barriers for the paparazzi, fans may perceive these acts as selfish and unappreciative. This is simply because they have an expectation level based on the celebrity's success that they should fulfill certain public duties.

Dealing with varying expectations comes down to the conflict between selflessness and selfishness. This is a complicated dilemma. You may selflessly strive to meet expectations in order to avoid disappointing others, but at the same time you selfishly want to honor your own needs and desires. At times it may feel like you are constantly having to choose between two roles: the superhero or the superservant. As a superhero, validated by your high levels of accomplishment, you may believe that you are extraordinarily capable of meeting all expectations. In doing so, you sacrifice your own needs and ultimately pay the price on a personal level. On the other hand, as the superservant, you may feel constantly indebted to others, therefore perpetually compelled to meet their expectations. As a result, you over-commit yourself and neglect your own needs. In both cases, the degree of selflessness is exaggerated due to how we define success and how we perceive our ability to maintain success. Over the long term, neither of these perspectives is healthy.

Expectations shape how we perceive experiences and our level of satisfaction in general. Certainly increased expectations occur with higher achievement, and meeting some expectations are important in order to continue along the path of success. However, these expectations must be managed effectively by walking a tightrope between degrees of selfishness and selflessness. By choosing how to respond and behave based on internal motivations that healthily define success, we can identify, understand, and prioritize expectations properly. We will never be able to meet everyone's expectations, and therefore we must identify which ones are reasonable and which ones are not. Fulfilling some while still attending to our own core needs is essential in properly managing the pressures of success.

PROJECTIONS AND FALSE CHARACTERIZATIONS

Reaching some level of success makes you a natural target of attention regardless of whether the attention is good or bad. Unfortunately there are times such attention is negative. A particular type of negative attention can be especially troubling: projection. In the purest sense, projection refers to the displacement of feelings and emotions from one person onto another. One person takes their own unacceptable motivations, desires, or traits and ascribes them to others. For example, instead of someone admitting they dislike another, they project these feelings onto the other person by believing that person dislikes them. While projection can occur with anyone or even a group, projection onto successful individuals is all too common. Not only are their lives and behaviors readily accessible to view, but ascribing negative projections onto high achievers serves to make some people feel better about themselves.

In some instances, projections onto high-achieving individuals are related to issues of power. If a person has problems with people in authority, negative perceptions will be projected onto anyone in such a position. Rather than actually examining the successful person as a human being, high-achieving individuals are assessed in terms of their role. By attaining a high status level in society, successful people are more commonly viewed from the perspective of the position—and then devalued—rather than being viewed for their actual personal traits.

Alongside projections are false characterizations. These occur when a person is given labels that are inconsistent with the truth. They can be used as a form of control or to generate news. We live in a fast-paced world and most people don't have the time or won't take the time to seek the truth. More often than not, social media, blogs, or tweets are quick to interpret actions and make judgments. Because there is less scrutiny, it is as if anyone can say anything without consequence.

For example, star athletes are often accused of not living up to expectations according to the role model status that society ascribes to them. But exactly what is a role model? By definition, a role model meets the expectations of a specific role. Therefore, if an athlete is a superstar basketball player, his role is just that and nothing more. His role as a basketball player does not include meeting expectations of being a parent, a businessperson, or a community supporter necessarily. Yet society frequently projects these additional roles onto successful individuals all the time. Unfortunately for high achievers, society broadens role expectations by projecting desirable qualities onto them that in reality may not exist.

In order to endure such irrational projections, you must constantly remind yourself that it is not about you; it is about the role or position you are in. Rest assured, that majority of people talking about you do not know you personally. So as hard as it may be, if they don't know you personally, then what they say shouldn't be taken personally. Easier said than done, but being unaware or unable to make this distinction can serve as a tremendous source of stress and anxiety.

LOSS OF AUTONOMY AND PRIVACY

Depending on your level of status and visibility you will invariably have to deal with people's desire to know more about you. The spotlight makes you a person of interest, and the feeling of ownership the public may feel it has over you can be quite uncomfortable. You may have heard some fans say, "I pay for the tickets and therefore his or her income." In essence, this perception that successful people owe the public something stems from a relationship of mutual exchange. Because the public has bestowed attention on the high achiever, they now feel entitled to receive something in return. Unfortunately for successful individuals, this demand may involve a direct invasion of their privacy.

The relationship between highly successful people and their fandom is quite vicarious. On the one hand, the sense of entitlement regarding access to details about public figures emanates from our capitalistic society. Society feels it has "paid" for the right to know more about one's personal life simply by granting that person a high status level. The successful individual should therefore oblige and provide access to the intimacies of their life as part of this fair trade. But this arrangement was never properly negotiated between the adoring public and the person of great success. Instead, it was simply assumed. Unless we appreciate that this is a presumption and not a legitimate demand, we can quickly give up our rights to privacy and suffer in the process.

Just as the public expects access to private details of people in the limelight, they also threaten to shun them if they fail to cooperate. This feeling of perceived ownership also grants them the notion that they can make or break a successful person. But this view has been repeatedly proven wrong. Consider celebrities who have protected their privacy despite their fame and achievements. How do we know they have done this well? Because we rarely hear about them in the media or entertainment news. In contrast, celebrities like the Real Housewives stars have embraced a complete loss of privacy by making their public and private lives essentially the same.

The challenge here lies in maintaining a distinction between your public and private life. When the lines between the two blur, problems can quickly develop. Worlds collide and private matters become exposed to public view, thereby creating additional stress and pressures. Everyone is entitled to a degree of privacy, and even the most successful people have the ability and right to protect confidential aspects of their lives from the public. Of course this takes effort, but it also requires an understanding that simply because the public demands information doesn't mean they are allowed to have it. Effectively defining the boundaries between one's public and private lives thus becomes an essential task on a regular basis.

TIME AND ENERGY MANAGEMENT

No matter what area of success is being considered, a certain level of energy is required in order to attain a goal. Each of us will be faced with a decision about how much time and energy we are willing to invest at different stages of the journey. When climbing the ladder of success, you accept that sacrifices will need to be made and that great effort will be required. But what about after you have "arrived?" Do you continue to invest increasing amounts of time and energy into the continued pursuit of higher achievement, or do you settle for what you have already attained and enjoy its benefits?

The choice is different for everyone. For many, negotiating a lesser investment of time and energy so that personal space and time can be enjoyed is often healthy—especially because it is these items that have likely been sacrificed for one's initial achievement. For others, a need for attention and the satisfaction of being in the rat race offers greater reward than the luxury of such space and time. Depending on how you define success, the amount of energy to be invested will vary.

Having an internal barometer of what matters most in relation to high achievement serves individuals well. When external rewards such as attention and fame are desired, the need for these rewards can drive one to expend energy and time past the point of what may be personally healthy. Ultimately, the costs may include broken relationships and a personal level of unhappiness. In some cases, continued effort and pursuit of success may result in public embarrassment and humiliation. This often happens with aging athletes as they attempt to extend their physical prime past the point they should. Instead of being remembered as one of the greats, they then become remembered as one of the broken-down has-beens. Not only did they fail to fully enjoy their time at the top, they tainted the public's view of their accomplishments by investing too much for too long.

When deciding how much to invest and how much time and space to allow for one's self, we might turn to the concept of Pareto efficiency for assistance. Named after the Italian economist, Vilfredo Pareto, this concept states that at maximum efficiency, investing greater effort into one area cannot be accomplished without significantly detracting from another area. The goal is therefore to reach the place of ideal time and energy expenditure by investing adequate efforts to meet one's inner goals for success while also allowing enough time and space for the enjoyment of what that success brings. Not only does this vary from person to person, but it also varies moment to moment. In order to properly manage this stressor of success, taking a continual inventory of what matters most and prioritizing become essential activities.

ROLE TRANSITIONS

The final stress discussed in this chapter involves the challenge of transitioning from one role to another. This transition represents how you move from where you were (culture of origin) to where you are now (culture of competition). Particularly in instances when success happens almost overnight, the pressures of making such a rapid transition can be overwhelming. Little time is available to contemplate what each role means and represents. It is therefore important to realize the inherent pressures this transformation brings.

The disjunction between the role one has served prior to success and the one after high achievement can present conflict and confusion. If you are entrenched in your role in your culture of origin, making this transition can be difficult. In order to survive in the culture of competition and success, you must learn to adapt to your new role. This seems simple enough, yet any change in your role has a significant impact

> You can change your knowledge, behaviors, and perspectives without changing the core of who you are—regardless of how others may perceive you.

on those around you. As we adapt to a new role, we naturally disrupt the roles of others in our lives. For example, a woman who primarily serves as a homemaker in her culture of origin may suddenly become the major breadwinner after achieving great success in her home-based business. This change in role affects all the other family members as a result. Another example of complex role transitions can be seen with children of immigrants. When parents do not speak the language of a new country they rely on children who have grown up in that land. The kids are then thrust into a leadership role that they may not be prepared for.

Adapting to a new role does not necessarily mean relinquishing your old roles completely. You can change your knowledge, behaviors, and perspectives without changing the core of who you are—regardless of how others may perceive you. Your inner values can still be consistent with what they were when you started the journey, and you can adapt to accommodate both old values and beliefs into the new role that success requires.

ONWARD!

The aforementioned stresses common to success pose major challenges for high performers, and failing to be aware of them and to understand the basic core conflicts involved can result in emotionally driven and poor choices. Such bad decisions result in dysfunctional behaviors that further complicate lives and lead to a declining degree of personal fulfillment. Despite what society would have you believe about success, the path toward high achievement is not the only place of significant struggle. Even after achieving your goals, you must continue to deal with persistent pressures and demands. The time has come to appreciate these challenges as you strive for even greater accomplishments, and to learn the skills needed to handle not only these stresses but also the challenges involved in managing the temptations of excess and increased access.

SKILL #1:
HANDLE THE "HARSH" TRUTHS

CONFRONTING THE HARD REALITIES THAT THREATEN TO KEEP YOU STUCK

"You can't handle the truth."
–JACK NICHOLSON

For all of you who saw the infamous scene in the film *A Few Good Men*, that line probably left an indelible impression. It has resonated through our culture over the last few decades, not only because of the emotional charge with which it was delivered, but because of how deeply it cuts to the core of our reality. It is a fact that there are some things in this life that are so painful or complex that it is easier not to address them. There are some things in life we just don't want to know. And the truth is that there are many things that we don't need to know. For instance, we don't need to know all the biochemical components of a medication or how an airplane is constructed in order to reap the benefits. However, when it comes to surviving success, the saying "what you don't know won't hurt you" is only half of the story. In my experience, "it is what you do know but refuse to confront" that can be the most damaging. It can be easy to revert to a state of denial or avoidance, but ultimately there comes a point when you have to make a choice: to confront the harsh realities of life or not to confront them.

In this chapter, you will learn the importance of confronting the "harsh realities" because, in my experience, the origin of many of the disappointments and frustrations of high achievement are embedded within them. For all of the benefits that come with high achievement, there are a considerable amount of disappointments that also occur. These disappointments range from reality not meeting expectations to not getting the respect one feels they deserve. On many occasions, my clients wonder why they feel no different after they have accomplished their goal. They ask themselves the question "Is this it? This is what I worked so hard for?" Or they are in a state of disbelief that they will continue to have to deal with the same type of problems they faced along the way to their success. They will—the only difference is that the stakes are now higher. In addition to the surprising disappointments are the nagging frustrations that seem to escalate the higher one ascends. These frustrations often deal with unresolved intrapersonal and interpersonal conflicts.

> In my experience, "it is what you do know but refuse to confront" that can be the most damaging.

The harsh realities are the facts that we consciously or unconsciously perceive as too confusing, painful, or time-consuming to address. Consequently we are tempted to skirt around the issues, hoping that they will magically disappear. More often than not they catch up to us at the most inopportune times. For years I have worked with individuals who have struggled to face the harsh realities of this world. Either they try to avoid them or they try to use their strengths and finances to overpower them, only to find themselves frustrated, overwhelmed, devoid of energy, and suffering unnecessarily. Unlike a Hollywood movie however, when it comes to you and your journey, you don't always have the luxury to avoid what you might find unpleasant. Yet it is imperat to ongoing success that you identify and confront these challenges.

The harsh truths are difficult to face because they threaten to destroy the fantasies we construct about the world. We create mental images of how we want things to look in a manner that gives us just the right motivation and drive we need to make those things happen. However, there are certain things that are beyond one's control or are not feasible due to timing and resources. Clients of mine who find themselves perpetually frustrated with some relationships or responsibilities, or feel constantly disappointed or let down, are usually bumping up against one of the universal truths that serve to entangle many high achievers.

Why face the harsh truths? So you can stop pretending and make better use of the energy you previously used toward maintaining a façade. It enables you to stop wasting time, knowing that where there is no truth there is no traction. When you learn how to handle the harsh realities, you can generate real

> The harsh truths are difficult to face because they threaten to destroy the fantasies we construct about the world.

momentum that withstands the inevitable tests that success brings. The key point to recognize here is that the way is through the pain, not around it. All that said, here are the top five universal/harsh truths that plague high achievers.

HARSH TRUTH #1:
"THERE ARE NO ABSOLUTE GUARANTEES."

Success has a way of conditioning us to think that, as long as we work hard, things will always work out in our favor. The truth is that no matter how far you have come or how things have unfolded to this point it is not definite that things will continue in the same manner. I say this not to be cynical but to help you to stay focused. There are no guarantees that people will show you love and respect now that you have been promoted. There are no guarantees that because you have had a stellar track record that your next season or idea or will be just as successful.

Knowing this, expert marketer and featured on ABC's TV show, Secret Millionaire, James Malinchak, takes nothing for granted. In an era where many workshop leaders are struggling with low attendance rates, James's "Big Money Speaker" workshops are

> Trouble often occurs when you are holding on too tightly to "what was" rather than facing "what is".

constantly sold out, with up to 800 people in attendance. Never resting on his laurels, he often states, "I don't know one way to get five hundred people into the room, but I know fifty ways to get ten people there, and I use all of them." James knows what many other highly successful individuals need to understand: Success has a tendency to breed complacency. To rest on your laurels marks the beginning of the end.

Keeping this truth in mind will also keep you protected. It can serve as a buffer against the inevitable tragedies that life brings. When something drastic happens, such as a lawsuit, a betrayal, an accident or unexpected economic shift, it has the potential to shake your whole foundation. These events can be devastating, especially if you have had all your eggs in one basket or have had an intense attachment to the desired outcome. With so much invested, it naturally feels harder to bounce back. Trouble often occurs when you are holding on too tightly to "what was" rather than facing "what is." It is this type of relentless attachment that becomes a clear recipe for perpetual resentment and disappointment, which easily becomes the emotional baggage that hinders your growth.

Remember that in life the only guarantee is you will have to work and continue to work to get what you want. As long as that remains your significant and consistent focus you are destined to win far more than you lose. And if you do lose, you will always have the option to cut your losses and get back to work.

HARSH TRUTH #2:
LIFE IS STILL NOT FAIR.

Bill Gates has been attributed to the following quote from a high school commencement speech: "Life is not fair. Get used to it." And he is right. For the high achiever this unfairness of life has a special twist. It could be seen that it is not fair that you got accepted into that great school and your equally smart friends didn't. It is not fair that your parents worked and sacrificed ten times more than you and you make more in a year than they made in their lifetime. It is also not fair that no one understands how hard it is for you. No, it is not fair. It wasn't fair back then and it's not fair now. And to top it off, it also isn't fair when you are denied opportunities because of your success, either because you threaten other individuals or because you have been judged as not having achieved enough. No matter how high we climb or how talented we think we are, the fact remains that there will always be someone faster, stronger, smarter, richer, more connected, or

> There will always be someone faster, stronger, smarter, richer, more connected, or better looking.

better looking. It's a fact of life. This truth can be exceptionally challenging to face because the higher you rise, the
more intense the competition becomes. There is a natural
tendency during such competition to gauge your progress by
comparing yourself to others. Instead of focusing on your
tasks you may find yourself constantly looking over your
shoulder to see what everybody else is doing or possesses. If
you sense that you are coming up short, the mind can quickly
go into justification mode, which in turn causes one to start
playing the blame game.

Instead of getting stuck in the
cycle of constantly looking for the
fairness in situations, just realize
that life is not always going to be
fair. In fact, constantly looking for

> Compete but
> don't compare.

fairness can be a waste of valuable time. Now, this doesn't
mean you shouldn't fight for justice, but that is a whole other
discussion for a different time.

Resist the urge to indulge in constant comparison. Instead
of wishing the world were more fair, spend the time looking
for ways to become more competitive. I firmly believe we
all have a unique formula of skills, knowledge, and available
resources that perfectly suits our ultimate destination. The
key is to find and consistently use these advantages instead
of taking inventory of someone else's skill set or attempt to
apply someone else's formula. Your path is yours. Theirs is
theirs. In other words, compete but don't compare.

HARSH TRUTH #3:
IT WILL NEVER TURN OUT EXACTLY LIKE YOU EXPECTED.

We are driven by the fantasy of what things will look like

when the new job is obtained, the contract is signed, c degree is earned. We imagine the celebration, the rec tion, and the respect. Of course everything is going to get easier now that you have more money and power, right? Little did you know that the celebration was going to be short-lived and most of your energy would have to be spent learning how to deal with obnoxious uninvited guests to your victory party. Instead of finally feeling free, you feel as if all kinds of strings have been attached. Instead of more autonomy, you are now at the whim of the puppet masters of greater expectations and increased responsibility. The celebratory mood quickly darkens into an atmosphere of survival.

Holding onto a fantasy can destroy you. As you climb the ladder the view naturally changes. When the view changes, your perspective changes. When your perspective changes, possibilities change. When possibilities change, your course changes. When the course changes, the destination changes. Remember, just because you

> Motion breeds clarity, which leads to the course corrections that place you in alignment with what is most important to you.

wanted something to look a certain way doesn't mean that it was supposed to look that way. An expanded view is a healthy sign of growth. Be careful of constantly trying to contort everything to exactly how you want it to be. Remember, it is not so much about the destination, but rather your direction. Motion breeds clarity, which leads to the course corrections that place you in alignment with what is most important to you. If you find yourself constantly bumping up against a wall, remain open and flexible, recognizing that some things are meant to be appreciated as they are, rather than controlled.

HARSH TRUTH #4:
YOU CAN'T PLEASE EVERYONE

You may have been familiar with this truth for some time, but somehow, as a result of your success, you have begun to feel pumped up by validation. Now you feel like you can conquer just about anything in your way. And perhaps you've convinced everybody else to feel the same way about you. As a result, the more you achieve, the more those around you may feel that it is alright to demand things of you. After all, "To whom much is given, much is required," right? Be careful of running here and there, constantly trying to meet everyone's needs. Most of the time, this drive doesn't originate from generosity but from guilt. No matter how much you give or to whom you give it to, it will still somehow feel that it is never enough. Guilt will make you hypersensitive to disappointment. Consequently, guilt-driven behaviors will land you into an endless cycle of unhealthy giving that could be detrimental to you and others.

Generosity can be a double-edged sword, especially for the high achiever. There are times when your generosity will not meet the expectations others have of you. Whether it is your attention or finances, there is always the potential that someone will feel shortchanged. Ironically, when you spend time in one place, the people in another place get upset. You finally get out of the neighborhood and now you are accused of thinking you are "better than." You move into a new part of town and feel treated like you are "less than." The list goes on and on.

At some point you realize that no matter what you do, somebody, somewhere, will find fault with you or choose to perceive you in the wrong way. Learn to let go of the guilt and frustration this can cause. Recognize that not only is there a natural tendency for us all to prioritize our own needs over others', but we are also not always rational in our requests. Be careful of hoping that people will totally understand. They won't. Learn to determine when the pull of the requests starts to become too much. Be especially careful of the tendency to fall into passive aggression by running yourself into the ground, thinking that now people will understand the pains of their requests. Some will, but most won't.

HARSH TRUTH #5:
THE WORLD DOESN'T OWE YOU.

Also known as "It's not personal, it's business," this truth is probably one of the most difficult to reconcile. Why? In order to get where you are, you have likely had to dedicate hours and hours of your time and energy for so many years it's hard to count. You have worked hard to make your company profitable and your teams better. You have worked hard on your sermons, albums, or publications. All along it has felt like you are not only striving for yourself but making significant sacrifices for those you serve or for those you plan to help. Your journey becomes very personal. So why does it feel at times that what you do or have done is not appreciated? You ask yourself, "How could they even consider trading me from the team or downsizing me? Don't they realize how much I have invested and sacrificed?"

As hard as it is to swallow, no matter what you think, results rule the day. More specifically, we live in a "what have you done for me lately" world. Whether you want to believe it or not, you are replaceable. It's just a fact. No matter how good you are or have been, if you don't produce, the survival of a business, team, or school depends on finding someone who will.

; was one of the most freeing revelations in my own jour-
I recall early in my training going to one of my mentors to complain about my situation. I told her that I had been recruited because of my unique talents and contributions, but now that I was here I was struggling with not feeling valued at all. In actuality I wasn't just struggling, I was upset and felt I had been duped. In her infinite wisdom, she sat me down and looked me straight in the eye. In a matter-of-fact tone, she said something that would permanently alter my perspective and my future. My mentor, a highly respected and decorated member of the organization, said to me, "Tim, no matter how much you have done, or how good you think you are, this place doesn't need you. Yes, it may be nice to have you here, but it doesn't need you. Remember, this organization was here before you got here and it will be here after you are gone." As I sat stunned by her bluntness, it clicked! What she was trying to help me to see was that I was spending way too much time and energy seeking validation. I was trying too hard to make the organization recognize and value me rather than spending time recognizing the scope of my opportunity and learning how to leverage it. The organization wasn't holding me back. I was the one holding myself hostage. But now I was free. The rest is history.

> "I was trying too hard to make the organization recognize and value me rather than spending time recognizing the scope of my opportunity and learning how to leverage it."

The key here is to always keep the big picture in mind. Don't over-identify with your position, status, or title. Use your opportunities to invest in things that are self-sustaining, such as education, experiences, and relationships. Know that the tides of life will inevitably change, and it is your task to be prepared when they do. These are the times when this change happens

> True traction in life comes from going through the truth, not around it.

instantaneously. Gone are the days of receiving a gold watch for forty years of service. Instead of waiting in expectation for acknowledgment that may never arrive, your task is to keep working hard at adding value. Invest in yourself, and remember, you are and will always be your own greatest benefactor.

SUMMARY

The harsh truths were hard to get around when you started your journey, and they remain so now. These realities represent universal laws that cannot be avoided if you want to remain at the top of your game. Wishing things were different doesn't cut it—but facing reality does. True traction in life comes from going through the truth, not around it.

STRATEGIC QUESTIONS

1. What areas of my life are the most frustrating?
2. What am I holding on to that is no longer serving me?
3. What realities do I need to face?
4. What is it costing me to avoid what I need to confront?

SKILL #2:
BREAK THE BOX

EXPANDING HOW YOU DEFINE YOURSELF AND SUCCESS

"Reality becomes a prison to those who can't get out of it."

–JOYCE CARY
(ENGLISH WRITER, 1888–1957)

"Never settle for being underestimated, under-valued, or marginalized"

–JOE MADISON 'THE BLACK EAGLE'
(RADIO HOST AND ACTIVIST)

I once attended an art festival in the desert and one of the exhibits was a man sitting in a large glass box the size of a small room. He sat in there for days. The statement he was trying to make left itself up for interpretation, as is the case with all forms of art. I, along with the others, marveled at the sight and tried to understand the meaning. At first it seemed fascinating and admirable. There were so many observers giving him so much positive attention and gifts. But as the days passed my perspective began to change. Was this glass box a showcase or was it a sanctuary- a private space of sanctity that enabled him to still see the world? By the end of the week my view had done a 180 degree turn, for I was convinced that what I was witnessing was, in actuality, a glass prison. In my mind he wasn't keeping us out—the glass was keeping him in.

Success is very much like this glass showcase. It's a special type of glass box that can illuminate, protect, and imprison you simultaneously. The higher you rise, the more visible and admired you become. At the same time, success isolates you, thereby validating the truth that it is lonely at the top. While those on the outside may admire or envy, the person inside the case finds it uncomfortable and hard to breathe. The increasing pressure and lack of oxygen can drive one to eventually act out in desperation. We don't have to look too far to find evidence of individuals trying to liberate themselves. Take someone like the child star who gets featured all over the media for self-destructive behaviors and legal violations—is this a form of acting out due to entitlement, or are these cries for help? And before him it was another star, and before her yet another . . .

Before we lean too hard on the celebrities, let's realize that the glass case phenomenon occurs at every level. Take the CEO who was recruited from a competing company. The organization is excited about the new acquisition and the potential for this person to come in and turn the organization around. Shareholders are comforted and stocks reflect a favorable public opinion. In essence the CEO is in the positive spotlight with great compensation. However, the flip side is that she discovers that the risk-averse culture is so restricting that she will not be able to make the immediate changes expected. She will have to make hard decisions that could result in the termination of some of those who are currently cheering her on. With so much faith placed in her abilities she begins to feel the true weight of her task. The glass case starts to feel lonely. As the oxygen level lowers, doubt begins to creep in and she wonders if she has been set up to fail in some sort of backroom political way. The box is beginning to take its toll.

The glass case is not all bad. It can serve as protection. Your title or talents can position you in a way that you don't have to deal with unnecessary challenges. For instance, if you are a graduate student in a demanding university training program, there is an inherent understanding that you will be spending a lot of time at school studying. In a case like this, people may very well check themselves regarding their demands of you.

The box can create efficiency. Your title or the role you play has already been defined and you don't have to waste time, energy, or heartache trying to figure it out. "Do your job" is one of the phrases that the highly successful New England Patriot organization uses as its slogan. This simple motto gets straight to the point and helps the members to stay focused. You were recruited for this job. The job is clearly defined. The expectation is that you will do that and nothing else to the best of your ability.

If there are multiple benefits to the box when should one be concerned? As we have seen, the box represents a degree of confinement one experiences with higher levels of achievement. It also represents conditioned ways of thinking and behaving that have outlived their developmental purposes and now pose significant barriers to necessary growth. In both cases, the glass box has gone from being helpful to being a hindrance.

Some other signs that may give you a hint when the showcase has turned into a prison:

- You feel suffocated or restricted in a way that impedes your personal or professional growth.
- You feel you are constantly repressing who you are and suppressing what you feel.

- You feel as if you are constantly pretending, which in turn is causing an immense amount of stress.

- You are trying too hard to fit in while knowing that you likely won't ever fit in, and frankly you don't really want to but feel that you must.

- You find yourself resentful or envious of others who appear to be free.

The metaphorical box for the high achiever isn't a result of a spontaneous external force, but rather a co-creation between you and your environment. Knowing how it is formed will help you. A better understanding in this respect will not only help to free yourself from its confines but also prevent you from creating other boxes in the future.

THE FOUR WAYS YOU GET BOXED IN:

INTERNAL PERCEPTIONS: HOW YOU DEFINE YOURSELF

In life, how you see the world will shape how you react to it and determine what you think is possible. This is especially true for how you perceive yourself. Perceptions are primarily shaped by what you have seen, heard, and experienced. Through all of your experiences, both good and bad, it

> How you label yourself can be liberating or limiting depending on the environment, demands, and responsibilities.

will be what you have internalized that will serve to shape how you view yourself and your world. We box ourselves in when we hang on to outdated or limited labels that derive from our perceptions, which may in fact be misperceptions.

How you label yourself can be liberating or limiting depending on the environment, demands, and responsibilities. The key thing to remember is that the label you give yourself will determine what and who you prioritize. For instance, notice the mindset shift of saying "I am a basketball player" versus "I am a student-athlete." Or perhaps, "I am an executive" versus "I am a father." In the entertainment world, "I am an actor" works well in the Hollywood scene. However, it may not serve you well if you are applying for a job as an accountant. We all have different roles we play in life, so the labels we are assigned are not mutually exclusive. The point is to be cognizant of the primary label you are relying on. If it has become too confining then it may be time embrace a broader and more empowering perception of how you see yourself.

EXTERNAL PERCEPTIONS: HOW OTHERS DEFINE YOU

There will be multiple reasons why people define you as they do. However, in the competitive world there are two primary ways that will shape how you are viewed. The first is by your status—that is, your title, affiliations, or accomplishments. The second way is through your behaviors. Although first impressions are powerful, how you consistently act will cement public perceptions. If your behavior is inconsistent with your position it can become fodder for people to make global judgments about you. In the world of social media it can be especially hard to bounce back. Negative external perceptions are hard to deal with because it can often feel as if it is beyond your control. We have ample evidence of how one "Decision" can turn an entire city against you despite years of service.

PERSONAL EXPECTATIONS:
HOW YOU DEFINE SUCCESS

How you define success is largely dependent on not only your own ideas, but also the ideas you have borrowed from influential people in your life. If you tend to see things with a narrow view, this will be a set-up for failure. For example, if you define success only in financial terms such a definition may cause you to make major sacrifices in relationships and other opportunities that you will later regret. I have found that we get boxed in not only by borrowing expectations but by setting unrealistic expectations that make us feel perpetually "less than." It is true that we often live up or down to the expectations others have of us. But what about the ones we have for ourselves? Suppose we have expectations of success that are too high. If you define success only by winning a Super Bowl or the Nobel Peace Prize and it never happens, does that make you a failure? If we view success as represented only by a lofty and nearly unattainable level of achievement, we will demand perfection from our efforts in order to reach this level of achievement. While this approach may encourage great accomplishments, in the end those expectations will serve to be self-destructive. Because our expectations are so high, we will most often fall short, which directly attacks our self-image. We develop anxiety that we will never be "good enough," and our self-esteem is negatively affected. In essence, we sabotage ourselves simply by developing standards of achievement that are unrealistic. As a result, we are unable to personally grow in a direction that is healthy and fosters true success.

> We get boxed in not only by borrowing expectations but by setting unrealistic expectations that make us feel perpetually "less than."

PROFESSIONAL EXPECTATIONS:
HOW YOUR JOB OR POSITION DEFINES SUCCESS

This is something that you need to know right up front. Every job has its requirements and behaviors that someone expects to coincide with your performance. Much has been written on executive presence, which helps others feel confident in your leadership. How we get boxed in here is when we feel stretched too far outside of the areas of our key strengths. Take for instance the top sales person who now gets promoted to a manager. The job is no longer about closing the customer, now it is managing people and resolving conflicts, responsibilities that require a different set of skills.

Or perhaps you are an athlete who has played one position all of his life, but now has to learn a new position if you want to get any playing time. Sometimes the professional expectations extend beyond just learning new skills. Sometimes you get boxed in by having to deny a significant part

> It is extremely difficult to sustain top performance if you feel like you are constantly losing a part of who you are.

of you in order to fulfill your new duties. This can be based on religion, ethnicity, or sexual orientation. It is extremely difficult to sustain top performance if you feel like you are constantly losing a part of who you are.

These are four of the ways that we create a glass box that slows or stunts our rate of growth. So what are ways to break through these self-imposed barriers? The following are strategies I have encouraged my clients to utilize over the years.

KEY STRATEGIES FOR
BREAKING OUT OF THE BOX:

1. **Define success based on your values.** Self-discovery is essential to developing an accurate definition of success. Even if we have been following someone else's vision of success, we can still correct our course by assessing whether our current direction matches who we are. Does our vision of success portray the things we find most important in life? Unless we ask such questions, we may ignore the things that bring us the greatest satisfaction. By reflecting on who we are as individuals, we gain insights into what type of achievements we most value and enjoy. This should be our starting point for developing an accurate definition for success. In order to best define success according to our own values, an effective strategy involves asking yourself the right questions that challenge you to slow down and think. In my experience, three probing questions have proven to be particularly powerful; asking ourselves these questions periodically as they relate to our goals and achievements provides us with a better perspective of how we characterize true success.

   a. The first question is "Who am I?" While it may seem mundane, the power and significance of this question is the most important in developing a definition of success that guides our behaviors. Unless we truly know who we are, we cannot establish the features that identify great achievements for ourselves as individuals. For example, I may care very little about being in the limelight or on stage because such things have little importance to me. But making a positive difference in many people's lives may mean a great deal to me. Knowing this about myself, my definition of success would be more likely to involve goals that make a large benevolent impact regardless of whether or not social recognition is present.

   b. The second question is "Am I who I say I am?" After going through a process of self-discovery, the next question addresses congruency. Do my actions and behaviors reflect the person I am and who I want to be? When we adopt other people's definitions of success, incongruence can exist between our own principles and our accomplishments. We might be well aligned with their dreams of achievement, but we are off course when it comes to our own perspectives. Determining if we are congruent with our inner values provides us with insights about how well we have thought about our goals for success. This may provide the first clue that our definition of success is off base.

c. The final question asks, "Am I all I can be?" Because the act of defining success is an ever-changing endeavor, we must regularly inquire whether our current definition is allowing us to reach our full potential. If we have expectations that are too low, the criteria by which we establish goals may limit our ability to grow as individuals. If we ask whether we have actualized our potential to the greatest extent, we will find multiple opportunities to refine our definitions of success to encourage personal growth. This enables us to take on new challenges, learn new skills, and achieve even greater accomplishments, thereby providing us with a deeper sense of fulfillment.

The three-fold strategy of self-discovery, congruence assessment, and self-actualization is an effective way to ensure we are constantly developing accurate criteria for defining success that meets our own needs and not someone else's. These questions allow us to define ourselves instead of being defined. Likewise, they enable us to change our definition of high achievement as we change and as our environment changes. And finally, they encourage personal growth. The solution is quite simple, and the questions are very straightforward. All it requires is an investment in time to self-reflect and the courage to act on those answers in order to better align our definition of success with who we are.

2. Shift from a static to a dynamic definition of success.

When asking individuals who have attained great success about their favorite part of the experience, they respond that it wasn't the attainment of a goal or completing a particular accomplishment. Instead, they reply the process of attaining success and the road to their achievements provided the greatest enjoyment and satisfaction. In other words, they were most happy when they were immersed in the flow of pursuing success. If we keep this perspective, we are more easily able to refine our definition of high achievement each step of the way.

Making this shift is largely a psychological exercise. It is about changing the context for which you see yourself and your role. Take for instance the parable of the stonecutters who were asked what they were doing. The first one said, "I am hammering this rock." The second one said, "I am molding this rock to be used for a wall." The third one stopped and looked to the sky and said, "I am building a cathedral." They were all doing the exact same thing, but which description is more motivating and likely to withstand the challenges that will inevitably come? Context is everything. Choose the definitions that activate you emotionally and guide you to bring out your best self.

(For more information about how to perceive progressive achievements as a continuum and as a journey rather than a destination, see the Conclusion to this book.)

3. Take advantage of change and transitions. Times of change provide the best opportunities to break out of a certain mold. Change brings on a natural disruption of conditioned patterns

> Context is everything. Choose the definitions that activate you emotionally and guide

of thinking and behaving. This disruption leads to greater openness and allows for individuals and organizations to be more creative. Transitions, such as the end of an athletic season, graduation, new jobs, or promotions, provide a window of time for you to take control of your narrative. Once you are clear on your values, take this time to both chart your course and manage your brand. What is most important to remember is that we play a large part on how we are perceived. Your patterns of behavior will be the strongest force that will either hinder or help the change you may seek. If you have been boxed in by negative or limited external perceptions of you, know that they can be changed over time. It is up to you to make sure that your actions are in alignment to how you desire to be looked upon or treated.

4. Create a space for yourself to play and grow. Despite its suffocating nature, there is always more room in the box. The question is what you will allow to fill it. Parkinson's Law states that work expands to fill the time available for its completion. This law also operates in our mental space. If we don't vigilantly protect that space, it is easily consumed by the demands of the day. Space can be of a physical or psychological nature. Examples of physical space include vacations, retreats, exercising, etc. Psychological space can be created through mindfulness and meditation exercises. Therapy is also a great way to obtain both physical and psychological space. The importance of the space is to suspend the normal pressures and demands of the day in order to connect with yourself or others in a way that fosters healthy growth. It is an opportunity to be authentic and vulnerable.

SUMMARY

In life we are often bound by both our personal expectations and definitions, as well as those ascribed to us by our public and professional worlds. Success has a peculiar way of requiring one to think and act in a certain way in order to replicate itself. Paradoxically it can lead to feeling and being perceived as one-dimensional. Limited definitions threaten to stifle growth and minimize perceived options. There comes a time when we have to expand beyond the exoskeleton of high achievement so as to experience new life. In doing so, breaking out of the box requires creating a space that allows you to connect and create from your core values, shifting from static to dynamic definitions, and taking full advantage of transition moments.

STRATEGIC QUESTIONS

1. Who am I?
2. Am I who I say I am?
3. Am I all that I can be?
4. What is the label or definition that I can embody that empowers me and brings out my best self?

SKILL #3:
TAME THE TIGER

HOW THE HIGH OF SUCCESS DISTORTS AND DELUDES

> "The enemy is within the gates; it is with our
> own luxury, our own folly, our own criminality
> with which we have to contend."
> –CICERO

Perhaps one of the best marketing slogans created over the last few decades is "What happens in Vegas, stays in Vegas." The campaign, run by the city of Las Vegas, embraces its unique culture and the fact that it is so different from the originating cultures of most of its visitors. The Vegas environment distorts perceptions and creates pressures that influence behaviors so that what happens there cannot be expected to be understood elsewhere. In the same way, success can be very much like a Vegas experience. Many successful individuals find themselves in a new environment with a multitude of unfamiliar pressures. And in this new culture, distortions occur about how one should behave. There's only one problem: Most of the time what happens during success doesn't stay as well compartmentalized as what might happen in Vegas.

One of the most successful shows in Las Vegas for many years was that of Siegfried and Roy. They were famous for their work with tigers and the show was said to have been seen by more than 25 million people. After decades of entertaining, everything came to a halt on October 3, 2003, when one of the beloved tigers attacked Roy, critically injuring him. Fortunately, Roy made a full recovery but the event was a reminder that even trained tigers and other animals of the wild can still be very dangerous if you become complacent or careless. The same can be said for success. It can lull you into thinking that the laws of nature do not apply to you.

The tiger that is success represents the "high" that comes with power and privilege. It is fed by glitz, glamour, favors and freebies. If one is not careful, it has the ability to distort how you see yourself and how you see others, and it can change what you value.

As we move from our cultures of origin to various cultures of success, different stresses and experiences naturally occur. These experiences influence us and mold how we act as a result. Without question, these adaptations can be challenging. For example, in our new culture of

> The tiger that is success represents the "high" that comes with power and privilege. It is fed by glitz, glamour, favors and freebies.

advanced achievement, we may be surrounded by decadence. Maintaining a sense of conservatism may be hard to say the least. If we allow our new culture to negatively influence our actions so that we betray our true selves, we may soon find we are becoming self-destructive. Identifying such distortions of our views of success and understanding how they occur are important in properly managing our achievements. Learning this lesson early can indeed save a great deal of misery later.

Social cognitive theory describes the above process quite well. As a learning theory of development, Social cognitive theory holds that environment (where we exist), behavior (how we act), and cognition (how we think) are all intertwined. For example, our environment influences how we think. What we think influences how we behave. And through our behavior, we receive feedback from our environment, which prompts our future decisions. This never-ending cycle of learning is constant regardless of whether we are successful or not.

In essence, we learn through observing others within our environment. When exposed to people who have attained high levels of accomplishment, we observe how they act, what clothes they wear, what interests they have, and so on. We naturally adopt similar behaviors if we wish to attain or maintain the same position as theirs. Likewise, we observe how others in certain roles think and what their expectations are. But what happens if those who we observe have behaviors and thoughts that are inconsistent with our values? In many situations of success, the environment and experiences are saturated with distortions, and these can lead us down an errant path.

The primary stress that occurs when we begin to reach higher levels of achievement involves a conflict between cultures. In the culture that we come from—our "culture of origin"— we became accustomed to certain thoughts, behaviors, and values. For most of us, this reflects our experience growing up with family and close friends. But as we begin to attain a higher social status or success levels, we are suddenly surrounded by a different culture. Because the new culture is relatively unfamiliar, we observe how others in this environment behave as well as their thought patterns. We naturally want to fit in socially with our new environment, so we take note of how others manage themselves. But when we must go back and forth between these two cultures, we may find an increasing disconnect between them. Negotiating the incongruence between these two environments and examining our behaviors and thoughts thus becomes a necessary task.

Adapting to new environments is a natural process for all of us. Over time, those environments and new experiences mold who we are. They change our perspectives and expectations. They influence how we think. Sometimes they pressure us to change our values in order to reach a compromise. For those who attain high levels of achievement, these pressures can be profound. We cannot escape the fact that we must decide how we will conduct ourselves in every given situation. But if we have poor insights about our need to skillfully negotiate our new environment, we can invite a distorted view and reaction to these pressures. For many, this is the major source of significant success-related problems.

FAILING TO TAME THE TIGER

In many instances, success breeds power and privilege. A celebrity actress suddenly has access to the finest restaurants and nightclubs in Los Angeles. A prominent sports figure becomes inundated with flirtatious women everywhere he goes. A congressman is repeatedly offered money in exchange for a desired political stance or vote. Regardless of what the appropriate response should be, the temptations that high achievement brings are new and powerful. When others within these environments succumb to these pressures without negative consequences, we may begin to accept a distorted view of what is acceptable for us within this same culture.

When we fail to tame the tiger of self-indulgence, we invite self-destruction into our lives. I often refer to this as the above-the-law mentality. We believe that our newly acquired level of success has awarded us a certain degree of immunity against the normal repercussions of bad behaviors. In part, this emanates from the environment itself. The nearly continuous exposure to selfindulgent opportunities begins to alter our view of what is permissible and what is not. In our culture of origin, a behavior may be completely forbidden and frowned upon, but in the culture of suc

> Success can breed a type of addiction not much different from other habit-forming behaviors and substances.

cess, it may be portrayed as normal and appropriate. Accepting the distortions of this new culture is what creates the problem. We lose the ability to maintain our core values and beliefs as we succumb to the pressures of hedonistic temptations.

Why can the indulgences of success be so powerful and tempting? Interestingly, success breeds a type of addiction not much different from other habit-forming behaviors and substances. The common pathway between the addictions of high achievement and those of drugs and alcohol lies in the production of a neurotransmitter in the brain called dopamine. Dopamine is a chemical involved in memory formation, learning, emotional responses, and in the pleasure-pain regions of the brain. When an individual takes an illicit drug the "high" or euphoria experienced is often a result of increased dopamine in the brain. In exactly the same way, indulgent experiences perceived as pleasurable cause the same dopamine release and can thus lead to the desire to repeat the indulgence over and over again. In addition, environmental cues (e.g., people, places, things) can play a large role in making one more susceptible to repeating addictive behaviors. Whether it be drugs, sex, pornography, or other indulgences, once the familiar characteristics associated with the experience return, a strong desire to repeat the habit appears. An environment of success that promotes self-indulgence is therefore no different. Taming this tiger can be just as challenging as controlling any type of addiction.

CHANGING SOCIAL RELATIONS WITH SUCCESS

While success often leads to environmental pressures that create distortions, changes in social dynamics can do the same. Inevitably, our relationships with others in our lives change when either we or they climb the ladder of high achievement. Demands, expectations, and commitments become different, and, as a result, the potential for stress in our relationships develops. The person of accomplishment is moving from a culture of origin to a culture of success that envelops him or her. But the solution is not simply moving from one environment to the other. Instead, we must find a way to effectively exist in both cultures. We must walk the tightrope and negotiate how we behave in both situations, while still being true to who we are as individuals.

Many of us have heard stories about someone from the neighborhood suddenly hitting the "big time" and having struggles with his or her existing relationships. Accomplishments have invited that person to take the next step forward while other acquaintances remain in a more static position. Social dynamics often change with success because the rates of personal growth and evolution differ. A steep curve of change is experienced by those attaining higher levels of achievement while the same growth curve for others is much more flat. In these situations, difficulties often appear in maintaining the relationships. Unless the relationship is blessed with a great deal of patience, insight, and understanding on both sides, stress and strain cause serious challenges.

Let's go back to our Vegas example to appreciate the environmental and social pressures of success. Imagine we have gone to Vegas for a long weekend to gamble and enjoy the entertainment. Within hours of arriving, we immediately begin to feel the cultural differences between Vegas and home. We're no longer surrounded by a mindset of clipping coupons and saving for a rainy day. Instead the new culture encourages spending money. In fact, money has a completely different value in this new culture. As a result of this different mindset and environment, a pressure develops for our own behavior to change.

From a social perspective, the people with whom we are now surrounded have embraced this new culture completely. Their mindset and behaviors provide us with examples that such a lifestyle is not only possible but pleasurable. Even if this pleasure is temporary, a lack of sustainability is hidden from our view. No longer influenced by the more conservative behaviors of home, we test the waters and begin mimicking these behaviors and indulgences. As we experience pleasure, we develop a desire to make this behavior more habitual. Depending upon how long we stay in Vegas, we may decide to convert over to this new culture altogether, leaving our old one behind simply because everyone else around us now operates by a new standard.

Success brings powerful experiences and social changes to our lives, and we must make hard decisions about the way we perceive our new levels of achievement as well as how we choose to think and act. The lure of self-indulgence provides the means by which the distortions of success develop. And if we fail to recognize these as challenges, then the consequences can be significant.

THE CONSEQUENCES OF DISTORTIONS

As individuals reach higher status, distortions of what their success means can create negative effects that have the potential to be quite embarrassing and sometimes devastating. We have ample evidence of how the media treats celebrities who "talk out of turn." We have seen political careers destroyed after statements that offended whole groups of people were made. We have seen sports figures say things and make decisions that have totally put off their fans. When this happens the disconnect between the two worlds becomes acutely apparent. Out of both frustration and disappointment, often both achiever and admirer will then retreat to their corners, resolved in thinking "obviously they (the other party) don't understand."

Environments of high achievement are intense. The obstacles that have been overcome to reach these levels are significant, and the pressures to maintain success are equally as powerful. Conflicts arise because cultures of origin and cultures of success are incongruent, often causing personal dissonance. As a result, consequences fall predominantly into two main categories. The first involves the development of bad habits while the second involves a shift in one's inherent values. When distortions of success are allowed to occur, these detrimental effects can occur. However, if healthy perspectives of achievement can be maintained, positive behaviors can persist, allowing for not only a measured enjoyment of success but its continuation and further growth.

DESTRUCTIVE HABITS

Distortions can cause a wide variety of bad habits. Perhaps the most common ones are financial. After attaining some level of success, many individuals easily adopt their new lifestyle, which allows them to spend more freely. But what happens when the degree of income decreases or the need to spend increases? When a distorted view of one's worth exists, spending may continue even in the face of declining revenues. This is supported by the countless number of ex-athletes and celebrities who have exhausted all of their wealth in the years immediately following their pinnacle of success. Unable to transition back toward a more modest standard of living, they continued to spend as if their success and income were untouchable. Clearly, these perverse views of their achievements and their inability to adapt to change create significant consequences that too often destroy everything for which they have worked.

Other destructive habits result from a need to "maintain the high" that success has brought. The adrenaline rush associated with fame and fortune may fuel other experiences that stimulate excitement and thrill. This can be something as simple as driving at excessively fast speeds to abusing an array of substances that create a temporary euphoria. The addictive tendencies sometimes associated with great accomplishments thus spill over into other areas. As a result, lifestyle habits that seek to re-create the distorted feelings attributed to success are embraced instead of the pursuit of healthier behaviors.

While excessive spending and reckless thrill-seeking are common destructive habits resulting from misplaced perspectives, numerous others exist. Some individuals take others for granted after becoming successful and treat them as insignificant. A false sense of self-worth develops that causes them to overvalue their own accomplishments and undervalue those of others. In other situations, individuals may mistrust others because of past experiences or because they fear being vulnerable to exploitation. Finally, some individuals begin to treat everyone around them in a businesslike fashion. Instead of characterizing their relationships with friends and family as special, everyone is lumped into a corporate-like category. Their mantra becomes "I'll do something for you and in return you do something for me."

What we don't often realize is how we treat others after attaining levels of success is an important reflection of how we view our own achievements. Healthy perspectives allow us to continue to value and treat others in a fair manner. By contrast, distorted views cause behaviors that demonstrate a misplaced sense of self-value or reflect bad habits in how we associate with others. An athlete may behave aggressively off the field instead of leaving such behavior "between the lines," or a celebrity may begin demanding services in public rather than simply on the film set. When these things occur, it signifies an inability to distinguish between environments. The same bad behaviors occurring in one environment are now occurring in others. Often these habits become so ingrained, we cannot properly adapt—not only between different situations but also over the course of our lives.

Consider a music production company back in the 1970s. As technology began to evolve, they continued to make vinyl records. Cassettes became popular, but the company continued to churn out vinyl. Then compact discs were in vogue, but they still refused to change. By the time digital music downloads were available, the production company was no longer around. They had gone from being incredibly successful to totally bankrupt simply because they couldn't adapt to their changing environment. Instead of shifting their paradigms to maintain success, they succumbed to a distorted view of what they thought was needed to compete. Successful individuals can wind up the same way when they remain stuck in their habitual way of doing things.

Underlying the negative behaviors related to distorted views of success are shifts in values. Rather than adhering to the internal values from which consistent actions should ideally be based, our values can gradually become influenced by the external aspects of a successful lifestyle. The most common distortion of values stems from the association of money with self-worth. How many times has the news informed us of some labor agreement dispute between a professional sports team and an athlete? Almost invariably, the terms of the dispute are related to money. Many times an athlete may even leave a city where he has established a strong sense of community simply because a team in another city offers a more lucrative contract. Many times this move backfires for the athlete, because greater importance has been assigned to dollars instead of less tangible things reflective of one's core values.

> The most common distortion of values stems from the association of money with self-worth.

While sports stars provide an easy example, the same can be said of any high-achieving individual. Money becomes the yardstick by which status is measured. One celebrity may balk at a movie contract if a rival actor has recently secured one for more money. A CEO may demand increased

> When these distortions occur, we no longer evaluate ourselves and our success based on the things that internally add importance to our lives.

salary and benefits before the corporate board if he feels other CEOs are being compensated with more. When these distortions occur, we no longer evaluate ourselves and our success based on the things that internally add importance to our lives. Instead, we externalize these values into financial terms. Ultimately, we sacrifice our true sense of self for one that can be traded on the market for a price. And even if we end up with the price we want, we might have already sacrificed ourselves and our happiness in the process.

Fortunately, the consequences of these distortions can be resolved if we simply step back and reassess what true success means to us. By redefining high achievement and envisioning our accomplishments as they pertain to us individually, we can establish healthy perspectives and habits while maintaining our core values. When this happens, we no longer give in to our self-indulgences because we are aligning our behaviors with reality and internal beliefs. This is the perspective we need to adopt a healthy view of success, so let us turn to the foundations of that perspective now.

KEEPING OUR FEET ON THE GROUND

When we attain high levels of accomplishment, we often receive constant positive feedback from others. Friends render their support and admiration. Family members brag about our achievements to their acquaintances. People we don't even know begin to recognize our efforts. All the while, our ego is enjoying the ride. But in order to deal with success in a healthy manner, we must keep our egos in check and our heads out of the clouds. If we don't, we risk developing detrimental behaviors, perspectives, and values from a perverse distortion of what is really true.

The first step in preventing a distorted view of high achievement is to stay connected to our inner values. These values may stem from our culture of origin—the fact of which does not require us to persist in that culture as success often does not allow it. Our values may have derived from mentors, education or faith experiences a bit later in our lives. Or it could be a combination of all these factors—in any case, the values we embrace should be able to persevere in any culture. This means constantly reminding ourselves of the things that are truly important such as honesty, integrity, humility, generosity, etc. By adhering to our inner values, we help deter the lure of self-indulgences that lead to adverse behaviors.

The goal is to negotiate any environment in a way that is conducive to our inner beliefs, but, unfortunately, many cultures of success do not naturally provide such an environment. Instead, we must create one that is not only healthy but also allows us to continue our successes. This is accomplished through three key efforts. First, we must connect to or foster an environment in which we can fully express our thoughts and feelings. In fact, distortions often develop when the ability to express ourselves is handcuffed. Second, we need to surround ourselves with authentic feedback. This is not the "yes-man" type of reaction that success often provides but instead critical and constructive feedback and support from those who are firmly grounded. Last, we must educate those around us about our experiences and cultural conflicts. This allows them to be part of the solution rather than part of the problem.

Below are four techniques for keeping your feet on the ground, while attaining high levels of achievement.

FOSTER THE RIGHT ENVIRONMENT.

The "right" environment will vary from individual to individual. In my experience the healthiest environments allow one to feel supported, validated, and challenged. The culture of competition has its own rules and priorities that may or may not align with what is truly important to you. Therefore, there is a considerable amount of vigilance required to protect what you value. The best way to do this is by being intentional about creating a healthy climate. For some this is achieved through connecting to spiritual communities on a regular basis as a reminder of serving a higher purpose. It can be achieved through meeting with friends, colleagues, and mentors who can help you keep a healthy perspective in times of stress. Regardless of the form that it takes, the magic is in being consistent. There will always be "good" reasons not to connect in this manner, so the best measure of action is to schedule it.

> The healthiest environments allow one to feel supported, validated, and challenged.

SEEK AUTHENTIC FEEDBACK.

Openness and expression are key ingredients to establishing healthy perspectives on accomplishment. This means not only expressing our own feelings and thoughts about success but hearing others' opinions as well. Real feedback and staying grounded in our values is important in this regard, and maintaining the ability to be open is crucial. While this sounds easy, the culture of success itself often prohibits such transparency and expression. In fact, high achievement may actually oppose such tendencies and be counterproductive to healthy behaviors.

Authentic feedback about our accomplishments is the easiest solution to prevent distortions. In some instances the environment of success in which we find ourselves can provide mentors who are willing to educate us about potential pitfalls. These individuals are excellent sources of critical and constructive feedback and also enable us to express our struggles along the way. In other situations, there may exist support groups composed of individuals who have had similar experiences. Through sharing and discussion, an accurate assessment of our position in life can be gained. Finally, professional advice is always available. Seeking guidance and recommendations from a psychologist, counselor, or psychiatrist familiar with the challenges of success is always beneficial. Regardless of which form of authentic feedback we pursue, receiving a reality check on a regular basis helps us to avoid faulty views of our own accomplishments. While we can still be proud of what we have achieved, we can avoid unhealthy distortions that overvalue our successes.

EDUCATE FRIENDS AND FAMILY.

In my experience, one of the most neglected solutions to prevent distortions involves the education of one's friends and family about the challenges of success. For me personally, the expectations surrounding me after becoming a physician were tremendous; and more important, my ability to express the challenges of my new status was limited. Family and friends need to understand the inevitable conflicts that arise when moving from one's original culture to one of success. High achievers are immersed in a sea of others' expectations, and indulgent opportunities are everywhere. Unless one's immediate support systems can appreciate these struggles, they too can become part of the problem.

Educating friends and families allows better self-expression and renders another opportunity for valuable feedback. The education of these individuals is important however because most will see at first only the benefits and not the pressures of high achievement. Involving a third party such as a therapist or mentor to highlight common stresses may be required because one's own ability to influence friends' and family's opinions may be limited. And while everyone doesn't have to understand, the most significant relationships should in order for us to be open with our thoughts and feelings. Through education and open dialogue, distortions soon evaporate, and we can then see what really matters.

MAINTAIN A GROWTH MINDSET.

In addition to creating a healthy environment, a key to staying grounded is remaining in a growth state of mind. Most of your achievements have come from the ability to learn and implement. As a result you were able to increase your capacity to problem solve and meet challenges. It doesn't stop after you have "arrived." The tendency in the midst of the chaos that success can bring is to avert your focus, either through "living the life," or managing the multitude of demands on your time and energy. Maintaining a growth mindset presupposes that there is room for you to get better and that it is possible. It is an acknowledgment that the conditions of the game have shifted and that there are new opponents with different tactics.

As we achieve success, maintaining a growth mindset becomes more challenging. During our initial climb to greater achievements, our motivations are oriented only toward success. We are willing to take greater risks, behave more

> Once we attain success our motivation changes...we begin to shift into a protective mindset to preserve

boldly, and fully express ourselves in our objectives. But once we attain success, our motivation changes. We no longer see attaining success as the only objective. Instead, we begin to shift into a protective mindset to preserve what we have already accomplished. Unfortunately, this naturally stymies growth, reduces our ability to take risks, and opposes our tendency to be open.

In order to maintain a growth mindset, we must be willing to constantly challenge ourselves. We should challenge ourselves to be open and transparent, to learn new things, to take ongoing risks in areas we feel are important for personal growth, and to have confidence in our own inner values and beliefs. By having a growth mindset, we are less likely to adopt distortions of what success means. Instead, we are more likely to adapt to an ever-changing environment through healthy perspectives of growth and openness.

SEEING THE TIGER FOR WHAT IT IS

Whether we have already attained success or are still striving toward our goals, certain distortions can occur that can cause serious consequences and problems. As we move up the ladder, we are tempted to take advantage of self-indulgences and feed our egos. Inner values are put on the back burner in exchange for temporary, material rewards. We begin to behave differently within our relationships. Before long, we adopt a false view of what is real and what success embodies. Only after reality comes crashing down do we realize how far off the real path we have strayed, and by then, it may be too late to recover.

The culture of success is one of high pressure and stress, and, unfortunately, managing these pressures can be difficult. If we lack authentic feedback and support to help us stay grounded, we can easily accept the distortions about success prevalent in society today. But by committing ourselves to a growth mindset and surrounding ourselves with realistic perspectives based on core values, we can keep a healthy view of what success means to us. With a healthy perspective, we can then establish reasonable boundaries that also align with our true goals in life. This is how we tame the tiger and align our actions with our beliefs, regardless of the pressures that high achievement brings.

SUMMARY

The "high" of success can be intoxicating to you and those around you. Unchecked, the power and privileges that you wield may lead to a distortion in values and behaviors that threaten to compromise your brand, your relationships and your health.

STRATEGIES

1. Stay connected to those that nurture a healthy self.
2. Seek authentic feedback and remain open to hearing what you need to hear and not just what you want to hear.
3. Educate and empower your support network.
4. Maintain a growth mindset.

QUESTIONS

1. What strategies do I currently have in place to help guard against distortions of success?
2. What strategies do I need to put into place?

SKILL #4:
LIMIT THE LOVE

HOW AND WHEN TO SAY NO TO YOURSELF AND THOSE AROUND YOU

> "Half of the troubles of this life can be traced to saying yes too quickly and not saying no soon enough."
>
> —JOSH BILLINGS

ncreasingly, people have spent more of their income and saved less over recent years. As an example, the recent crash in the real estate market illustrates how people have not only spent what they had but also what they didn't have. Banks were willing to finance the entire value of a home and, in some cases, extend mortgage amounts beyond the actual value. But when the market readjustments of the economic downturn occurred, thousands found themselves upside down in their mortgages, creating a wave of bankruptcies. Couples who were planning to retire and cash in their home equities realized such dreams were no longer possible. Because they had failed to establish healthy boundaries in their budgets, they found themselves in a position they never expected.

Likewise, the failure to set healthy boundaries is the number one reason success turns into failure. At each step of the way, we must establish limits on the pressures that others put on us and, more important, the ones we put on ourselves. The irony is that success and dependency go hand in hand. Although there are many hours spent alone working and grinding, it is true that "no man is an island." In order to succeed there is a level of reliance on others that is necessary. Typically what starts as an individual effort evolves into a community effort. As the game changes, other skill sets are required. If we don't have the necessary time or skill set then it is imperative that we recruit others who do have it. These are the people who can do what we can't do. They are the administrators, the publicists, the interns, the paralegals, the business managers, the hygienists, and the many others who play supporting roles. There is a natural dependence that occurs in these cases. Our achievements create opportunities, which turn into jobs, which represent people's livelihoods. These are the healthy dependencies that occur. They are mutually beneficial; there is a positive give and take. They also lead to greater levels of accomplishments.

> Achievements create opportunities, which turn into jobs, which represent people's livelihoods.

There is another type of dependence that can occur as one ascends to greater heights. These are the relationships both old and new that can feel as if they are taking more out of us than they are giving to us. We can describe these relationships as unhealthy in nature, characterized by manipulations, excessive demands, and the negative feelings they evoke. They have a tendency to force one to give out of a sense of guilt rather than authentic generosity. This type of dependence often leads to eventual downfalls, which, sadly, could have been prevented. More than ever it becomes paramount that we learn how to set healthy limits so that we no longer allow or develop toxic dependence on certain ways of thinking, unhealthy relationships, or material possessions.

BALANCING DEPENDENCE WITH SUCCESS

Success naturally creates dependence. This does not mean to imply that dependence is a bad thing in regard to success. Dependence is necessary and plays a unique role in the quest for attaining goals and accomplishments. A battle is constantly ongoing between our dependent and independent selves, and we must continually dance between the two in order to manifest our best potential. None of us achieve success in isolation. We all must rely on various people and situations to help us reach our goals. But becoming overly dependent on something by failing to establish a healthy boundary can be as detrimental to our achievements as being too isolated. The most effective journey toward success requires the critical skill of deciding upon whom and what we should rely and, most important, to what extent.

Dependence comes in a variety of flavors. We can be dependent upon the people in our lives who facilitate our accomplishments. For instance, an entertainer has to rely on a team of individuals to produce and promote his or her music. We can rely upon certain types of behaviors to achieve our goals. For example, we may rely upon a high-energy state to facilitate actions and behaviors necessary to meet the day's requirements. Many have become dependent on energy-enhancing substances for this reason as it allows them to

> A battle is constantly ongoing between our dependent and independent selves, and we must continually dance between the two in order to manifest our best potential.

accomplish more each day. It's no mystery why energy drinks have become so popular, but overdependence on such supplements has its downside. The "crash" after the substance wears off, sleep deprivation, blood pressure issues, and other health problems can develop as a result of relying too heavily on these energy-boosters.

What and who we depend on affects our attention and our actions. If we rely on a specific person to achieve our goals, we will constantly want to know where they are and what they are doing. We defer activities to them in order to meet our own objectives. If the dependency is a healthy one, then we accomplish our goals efficiently and continue to adapt and grow. But if the reliance is unhealthy, we may find we are unable to progress over time because we are stuck and unable to let go of what may no longer serve us. Trusting and depending on others helps us adapt and change to the world around us to a point, but if the reliance becomes too intense or excessive it becomes counterproductive. This is why establishing boundaries is so important.

PLACING LIMITS ON DEPENDENCES

Setting limits on dependence is important both for us and for others in our lives. Consider the family and friends of a well-known celebrity. As the celebrity becomes successful, these individuals may come to rely on her for financial support, professional connections, personal favors, and more. If boundaries are not well established, this dependence can quickly become harmful not only for the celebrity but for the ability of her family and friends to achieve their own autonomous success. Limits must be defined and consistently respected in order to create a healthy situation for everyone involved. Though some will never understand or appreciate the logic behind such boundaries, the effort must be made nonetheless.

Setting boundaries is essential and required of every individual who takes on more responsibilities or has to deal with competing expectations. Good boundaries help in several ways. They outline what we deem as acceptable behaviors. In other words, they teach people how to treat us. Boundaries help to define the nature of the relationship in a way that prevents role confusion. Good boundaries also protect us and provide us with space to grow. They can give us the time and energy to do what we want to do instead of constantly prioritizing the demands of others.

Self-discipline is a key ingredient for the establishment of boundaries that place us in the healthiest position to succeed. This means exhibiting restraint in our own actions while also ensuring that others around us realize what is and is not acceptable. We must be able to discern between positive and negative behaviors and situations. For example, not every opportunity to advance one's success is a good idea. Some will be positive while others will detract from our resources or prevent us from pursuing other key areas. Determining what is important to us by setting limits helps us negotiate which relationships and activities truly add value to our lives.

One client of mine produces a very successful entertainment event each year in the Southeast. Over the last decade, the show has grown tremendously in popularity and attendance. Over and over again, he has been encouraged to take the show nationally or franchise it. Despite the allure of that opportunity, my client made the decision to say no. If the event toured dozens of cities throughout the country, he would stand to make an incredible amount of money. But at the same time, he would need to be committed to the show twelve months a year. This would take him away from other interests and require he travel all the time. Additionally, he would have to juggle the increased responsibilities that his higher income, staffing, and event demands would impose. For his own personal goals, he has chosen instead to limit the event to its solo occurrence each year. In other words, he decided to say no.

In order to establish effective boundaries, we must understand exactly what our goals are within our area of endeavor and within our personal lives. For my client, being at home, having numerous interests, and having a manageable lifestyle are more important than increasing his fortune or notoriety. Because he understands his goals quite well, he is able to set limits that coincide with his life objectives. For many of my clients, this is not the case. They seek certain aspects of high achievement, such as wealth or fame, without considering what truly matters to them. As a result, their boundaries are loose, misguided, or even nonexistent. And as a result, they struggle to achieve the proper balance.

Setting limits effectively requires two key components. The first is self-respect. We must respect who we are as individuals. We each have specific needs and desires that allow us to maximize our potential. If we become overly dependent on wealth, for example, we may fail to respect our need for healthy relationships while we strive only to make more money. If we rely too greatly on an advisor to tell us what we should do, we fail to respect our inner voice, which actually knows us best. But if we have self-respect, we consistently take an inventory of our own needs and establish boundaries to protect those needs. In this way we avoid becoming overly dependent on things that are potentially detrimental.

The second component is self-discipline. Understanding our needs and having self-respect is important, but if we lack self-discipline, we may fall short in maintaining the limits we set. Self-discipline gives us the strength to say no to situations that are beyond our boundaries. Even if there are risks, such as losing an important relationship, our underlying understanding of what best suits us provides us the boldness and courage to enforce the limits we have established. Certainly there will be times when others do not accept our boundaries or even try to understand them, but ultimately the responsibility to hold steadfast to the limits we have established lies within us.

What we often don't realize is that we condition others as to how they should respond and react to us. For example, if we go to a party and approach everyone with a smile, a handshake, and a high degree of energy, we naturally invite social engagement, conversation, and dialogue. But if we attend the same gathering in a reserved fashion, existing in the corner shy and hesitant, others will react to us in a completely different way. The same applies when setting boundaries in our lives. We must show and tell family members, friends, colleagues, and others exactly what we are willing and not willing to do. In reality, we can only control our own behaviors and not theirs, but by consistently abiding by the same set of limits, others will eventually come to respect our wishes.

SEEING THE SIGNS

A prime example of overreliance on a skill set involves aging athletes as they near the end of their careers. Some have enjoyed more than a decade of high achievement and widespread recognition. They have been awarded fame and fortune while receiving a status the majority of us respect and envy. But if they have relied too heavily on their athletic talents without developing other skills to advance their level of success later in life, they may be lost when their physical gifts begin to decline.

Of course, overreliance on skills is not the only challenge for high achievers. Others come to depend on aspects of their past success in a way that causes problems for them later on. For example, those in the spotlight who receive the adulation of thousands may grow to be dependent on public recognition. As their success begins to decline, they may be unable to relinquish the quest to be the center of attention. Sometimes this leads to behaviors to gain attention at any cost—even negative attention. Why do so many ex-celebrities appear on reality television shows such as Celebrity Apprentice? For some, the incentive to raise money for a charity encourages them to participate, but for others, the ability to return to the public eye is what drives them to make the appearance. The individuals in this latter group may have become addicted to the rush to the detriment of developing other skills and talents to further ongoing achievements.

We may become dependent upon other areas of success, such as a specific lifestyle or income. Living in a stately mansion, driving expensive cars, and attending fancy galas can be falsely perceived as the means to continue high achievements. Instead of these aspects being viewed as secondary benefits, they become confused with the pathway to success. Because of this, individuals who have adapted to an elevated lifestyle and income can find it exceptionally difficult to adjust their behaviors after acute shifts in their financial state. Without some type of gauge to help them know when overreliance has occurred, they find themselves in a bad situation. For this reason, learning to look for tell-tale signs of overreliance or codependence is critical so that one's course can be redirected before it is too late.

What are some of the obvious signs that indicate we have become overly reliant and overly dependent? One of the most common is the presence of excessive worry. When we rely too heavily on something, such as an asset or a relationship, we naturally become concerned with the possibility that it might no longer exist at some point. Protecting our dependence then becomes our focus—in some cases, even our obsession—as we seek to control and preserve that dependence as if our lives relied on it. Why do you think some celebrity guitarists insure their hands? They see their continued success as dependent on this particular body part. In a similar way, some high achievers may offer valuable assistants large sums of money to stay with them because they see their future accomplishments as dependent on their daily support.

When taking an inventory of the items that account for our success, we should assess the degree of worry we assign to losing those things. The higher the degree of worry, the more we are likely to depend on them for future achievements. In some cases, some degree of concern may be healthy, but excessive worry is rarely beneficial to our long-term ability to sustain success. If identified, we should reassess why we feel so dependent upon that person or item and how we could adapt should it no longer be available to us. Alternatives are a great way to reduce dependence, especially if we begin to implement behaviors that make them viable options.

A second sign that might suggest overreliance concerns the amount of time we engage in a particular activity. For example, many Hollywood actors and actresses spend excessive amounts of time and energy on their physical appearance.

Similar to the athlete, youth has advantages for celebrities, and the battle to delay the effects of aging—which might start out as a wise career move—can quickly become an obsession. From overinvestment in exercise to plastic surgery, the amount of time (and money) awarded to these activities can signal an area of dependence and poor limit-setting.

Unfortunately, we may be oblivious to such disproportionate behaviors. We may justify our actions in a way that seems reasonable. For example, excessive exercise may be justified because of its beneficial effects on long-term health, even as the time we spend exercising robs us of time we could have spent in other important areas. Once again, taking an inventory of where we spend our time and energy can help us see potential areas of overreliance. Being attuned to what others are saying about where we spend our time can also be enlightening, because where we spend the most time almost always reflects what we value the most. Unless we take a good look at how much time we spend and where, we may remain ignorant to areas of overdependence.

While areas of worry and time investment can be early evidence of poor boundary establishment and overdependence, social problems and neglecting responsibilities are often the later signs. By the time relationships in our lives become strained, we have already spent too much time

> We sometimes need external "nudges" to help us wake up and to remind us of what we know to be most important to ourselves.

and energy in other areas for a while. Struggles with family, friends, partners, and colleagues can occur for a multitude of reasons, but overdependence is a common cause. If problems are beginning to occur socially, then an assessment of the root cause is an important exercise. Let's take the entrepreneur who finds herself spending an immense amount of time catering to her main client. As a result, her personal and home life begins to suffer. Subtle comments made by friends and family members about absences slowly turn into complaints and ultimately into major conflicts. In the midst of the work it may be difficult for her to take a step back and discern between what is appropriate and what is excessive. In these instances, we sometimes need external "nudges" to help us wake up and to remind us of what we know to be most important to ourselves.

The same, of course, applies to neglecting our responsibilities. Social responsibilities are one area of concern, but so are self-responsibilities and other commitments. Ignoring self-responsibilities can lead to unhealthy situations in which we eventually react to chronic areas of neglect. For example, sacrificing ourselves for a dependent relationship or behavior can lead to resentment and anger. Over time, these emotions increase and can ultimately cause us to lash out or behave in unacceptable ways. Similarly, failing to honor commitments reflects on our character, and no matter what level of achievement we have attained, being viewed as having a poor character can lead to bigger problems down the road. Disappointing those to whom we have made a commitment should be a red flag that we are either overextending ourselves or have become overly reliant on other items.

The solution to the problem of overdependence is the ability to gain balance. We must accept our responsibilities within limits while continuing to assign others their own responsibilities. We should constantly be willing to adapt and change along with the environment through the ability to let go of the old and invite the new, enabling balance and harmony through an ability to shift gears when needed.

SOLUTIONS TO OVERCOMING OVERDEPENDENCE

Setting boundaries is a necessary step in preventing overdependence on any one aspect of our success. In fact, sustained success demands we establish limits in a variety of areas so we may achieve the balance needed to continue our pursuits. Remember that areas of dependence shape our attention and our energies. If we become overly reliant on a single area, we become too focused on it to the point that hinders our attention to other important activities and relations. Ultimately, our ability to sustain the level of our accomplishments will decline as a result. Boundaries thus help us avoid the pitfalls of overdependence.

So, how is this accomplished? By taking inventories of areas where you worry excessively or overinvest your time, and by becoming aware of social problems and an inability to keep your commitments to others. One common denominator exists regarding effectively establishing boundaries. The key to success in setting limits depends on our ability to say one little word: "no." If we cannot master this simple task, then in all likelihood we will constantly struggle between codependence and overdependence. Realizing we do not have to embrace every single opportunity to be successful is what empowers us to turn away from situations where we will overextend ourselves. In reality, accepting every challenge is what will eventually spread us too thin and make achieving our goals impossible.

Saying no to some opportunities does not mean saying no to success in general—unfortunately, too many people believe this to be true. High achievers can come to understand that discernment is the primary skill they need. We must determine how much is too much and when energies going in one direction begin detracting from those going in another. Saying no is simply the means by which we achieve the balance we need to continue our success into the future. The aging athlete may decide to say no to investing more heavily in his physical skills and choose to work on his public speaking talents instead. As a result, he may be able to attain a broadcasting position after his sports career is over and sustain continued personal achievements.

Even when we establish boundaries, we can still enjoy a degree of flexibility. Because we are constantly adapting to a changing environment, setting limits too rigidly can be restrictive and can also hinder growth. By the same token, saying no to various opportunities does not always have to be conveyed in a highly assertive way. Different situations call for different ways of communicating a boundary. For example, some situations may demand an absolute refusal expressed in clear and certain terms, while other occasions may simply require more of a distraction technique. In one circumstance, we may need to blatantly say, "No, thank you," while in another we may politely say, "We are not interested at this time."

Determining how to communicate a boundary is a matter of social politics. We all have been approached by a salesperson who is never going to take no for an answer no matter how hard we express our resistance. We may then offer a disguised no by telling them we are interested and that we will contact them later or have someone else call them for the details. Though we are saying yes in order to escape the situation, in truth we are still saying no. There is an art of saying no in order to preserve our set limits and to avoid overcommitment or overdependence. This involves being direct, specific, patient, and consistent.

Establishing boundaries can also evoke emotions that make

it hard for us to protect ourselves. Most of us do not want to disappoint anyone regardless of how trivial their expectations of us may be, but if we give in to everyone's expectations, we soon find we are unable to enforce the limits we personally need. When we begin to say no to certain situations, we may feel guilt due to our own expectations of ourselves. We might feel shame or we might feel selfish. These emotions are all common and often a product of prior life experiences, but in order to adopt a more healthy perspective we must realize we cannot be everything to everyone. If we become dependent on pleasing the masses, we lose focus on our own goals and objectives.

Part of attaining great accomplishments is being able to adapt and grow; when emotions get in the way of setting healthy limits, we must acquire new perspectives. By understanding the dynamics between limits and dependence, we begin to see how overreliance and over commitment create obstacles to our progress. Sometimes we may learn this through difficult experiences, but in some cases we need help and support. If any of the tell-tale signs of poor limits and dependence exist, then seeking help from a mentor or professional may be the best approach toward balancing our lives most effectively.

DEVELOPING OUR OWN FEEDBACK SYSTEM

In medical school I learned a great deal about various feedback systems within the human body. For example, as we eat something sweet, the level of glucose naturally increases in the bloodstream. This rise then stimulates the release of insulin from the pancreas, allowing glucose to be absorbed by the body's cells. Once the glucose level in the blood falls, insulin production declines. The pancreas is thus always receiving feedback information about the level of glucose in the blood so it can adjust the rate of insulin production.

In regard to setting limits related to success, boundaries provide similar parameters for our own feedback system. If we exceed our boundaries for overdependence, we begin to invest too much energy and time into one area at the expense of others. If we become too codependent on another person for our achievements, we fail to grow and progress to our full potential. By educating ourselves about the signs of over-reliance, dependence, and codependence, we can recognize where limits need to be established. And by committing ourselves to those limits, we can have confidence in our ability to sustain success in the future. All it requires is the realization that through limits we gain balance, and through balance, we maintain the capacity to reach even greater accomplishments over time.

SUMMARY

The higher you rise, the more interconnected you become. To achieve continued success, you are now reliant upon systems and people who play specific roles. Success can foster a level of codependence that can take both healthy and unhealthy forms. Learning how to set appropriate boundaries is essential for your survival. Failure to set good boundaries typically derives from not only feelings of guilt, but also from fears of rejection and abandonment. Nevertheless, failing to set healthy limits can be detrimental to your physical, mental, and financial health.

STRATEGIC QUESTIONS

1. When do I need to say no to myself?
2. What boundaries do I need to set that would make my life ten times easier and less stressful?
3. Who am I enabling? Who am I empowering?

SKILL #5:
FOCUS YOUR FLOW

MANAGING DISTRACTIONS AND THE PRESSURE TO DO IT ALL

"A distracted existence leads us to no goal."
–JOHAN WOLFGANG VON GOETHE

n Survive and Advance, a film in ESPN's 30 for 30 series, the story revolves around the legendary NC State coach, Jim Valvano, who led his basketball team to the 1983 national championship over the favored University of Houston. It was a feat that captured the American spirit as millions around the country, including myself, jumped up and screamed as the game-winning dunk was slammed through the hoop at the last second. After that amazing accomplishment, the charismatic coach was inundated with media appearances and speaking engagements. The film makes mention that over time it was likely that these obligations began to take away from Valvano's coaching effectiveness and program oversight. Eventually the program became embedded in turmoil and controversy. Although never directly involved in any wrongdoing, the mounting pressure ultimately led to the beloved coach being asked to resign. In the end, Coach Valvano's legacy was not so much defined by basketball, but rather his courageous battle with cancer and the creation of the V Foundation for Cancer

Research (www.jimmyv.org). His story, however, serves as a reminder that, even with a giving spirit one can become susceptible to the pitfalls of a lost or diluted focus when pulled in too many directions.

As you climb the ladder of success, one thing is consistently apparent: Increasingly, everyone around you begins to demand more and more energy from you. You're a success, after all. If you are on your way to the top, other people will want to come along. If you have been proficient in one arena, others will assume your skills and talents extend into others. Before long, you are swimming in a sea of distractions, unable to stay on course. To focus your flow, you must learn to identify which activities in your life are well aligned with your success goals and which ones are distracting you from your real objectives. Attention is a limited resource, and allocating it wisely and productively by realizing how distractions creep into your life is essential for enduring success.

THE IMPORTANCE OF FLOW

The psychologist Mihaly Csikszentmihalyi popularized the concept of flow. In his book Flow: The Psychology of Optimal Performance, he describes flow as being a state of concentration or complete absorption with the activity at hand. He theorizes that it is in this hyperfocused state that people are happiest. The concept of flow can also be equated with the sports terminology of "being in the zone," where you are so tuned in that you effortlessly yield extraordinary results. The importance of the terms flow and being in the zone cannot be overstated. Their importance has often led to significant achievements and what is necessary to continue these achievements. Dr. Joyce Brothers has said, "success is a state of mind," and it is a state that requires a biological and psychological rhythm necessary to sustain it. Therefore, being vigilant about your focus is essential in minimizing the multitude of detractors that threaten to consistently take you off your game.

At this point in the discussion it is worth acknowledging the research on multitasking, which in itself can be a form of distraction. Multitasking may be necessary at times but also can create busywork that is not in alignment with your life's work. High achievers with multiple demands may seem to be doing multiple things at once, but it is actually far more likely that they are doing one thing at a time very well before switching their attention to doing another thing very well. Multitasking, on the other hand, has been associated with memory impairment, up to a 40 percent drop in work productivity, increased stress, and an increase in errors and accidents. In a recent New York Times article on multitasking the authors report studies suggesting that it can take up to twenty-five minutes for a worker to return to an original task after being interrupted. They also refer to a Carnegie Mellon study, in which subjects who were interrupted twice while taking a cognitive skill test scored 20 percent lower than the control subjects who were left alone. (Sullivan and Thompson. "Brain Interrupted." *New York Times* 3 May 2013). The results of these and many other studies highlight the need to be very discerning in what we decide to engage in or agree to. Under the guise of speed we could be unknowingly sacrificing efficiency and effectiveness, which can prove to be very costly.

> Multitasking may be necessary at times but also can create busywork that is not in alignment with your life's work.

EVER-INCREASING REQUESTS AND RESPONSIBILITIES

Often others assign us greater responsibilities as we begin to attain higher achievements in our lives. You may have experienced this at a very young age. A Little League slugger may be asked to steal second base in order to put his team in a winning position. A talented middle school drama student may be asked to play two roles in the school play because the talent pool is limited. An exceptional student may be asked to tutor one of her peers during class to assist a teacher with her educational duties. Assigning additional and complex tasks to others based on exceptional performance is natural and part of human behavior. And to a point, it can actually be beneficial in furthering your success.

However, at some point, too many responsibilities can begin to detract from your own goals and objectives. If the drama student has too many lines to remember for both roles, her performance in both casting parts may suffer. If the student spends too much time tutoring his peers, he may fail to excel in his own academic achievements. Being given greater responsibility can enhance self-confidence and also allow you to tackle new challenges, but no one's well is bottomless. No matter how skilled and talented you may be, at some point you exhaust your capacity to take on new roles and duties. If you extend yourself beyond your breaking point, every area of your life will then be negatively affected.

> As you are pulled in many directions, you soon find less time to spend on the activities most important to you.

Increasing responsibilities are thus the most common form of distractions related to high achievement. As you are pulled in many directions, you soon find less time to spend on the activities most important to you. The goals important to you may get confused with the goals of others. And in some cases, additional demands pose new challenges, for which you may not be prepared. When you allow success to influence your focus on what is most important and the nature of your true abilities, you invite distractions into your life. Distractions are the noise and clutter that keep you disorganized and prevent you from being efficient. In fact, being distracted is commonplace as you move up the ladder of success.

THE MYTH OF GLOBAL COMPETENCE

Being exceptional at one thing does not guarantee that the skills or fortunes will translate into other situations or areas of your life. Take, for instance, what happens to practicing physicians. Several of my physician colleagues have evolved in their careers as health care has changed. Increasing demands for more efficient delivery of services, lower costs, shortened hospital stays, and higher quality of care have created new roles for many doctors. Instead of performing patient-care duties, some were asked by insurance carriers and hospital executives to take on new responsibilities in health-care administration. Assuming their medical success in the clinical arena would translate into success in business management of health care, an expansion of responsibilities was requested.

At first glance, such an assumption might seem reasonable. After all, physicians are the ones involved in the day-to-day activities of health care, and so it only stands to reason they would be best equipped in seeing limitations and shortcomings. But just because doctors are proficient in providing medical care does not mean they are similarly proficient in allocating medical resources and running a business. In fact, do you know how many courses medical students are required to take to assist them with managing a medical practice or negotiating health insurance contracts? Zero. Why then would we assume physicians would automatically be equipped to be effective administrators?

Such assumptions are based on the idea that individuals' success in one field translates to other arenas as well. Certainly, in some cases, physicians have become excellent health-care administrators and business people, but this is not always the norm. In fact, physicians are stereotypically ineffective investors and entrepreneurs when pursuing areas of interest where they have little foundational knowledge.

The assumption of global abilities is not limited to others' perception of us. We also tend to accept this assumption of ourselves as we become increasingly successful. Our level of confidence grows with our greater accomplishments to the point that it can distort the reality of our own abilities. This false assumption of global competence can lead us to accept too many responsibilities, which in turn distract us from our primary objectives toward success. In some instances, we may lack the actual skills and abilities to perform at a high level in our new roles. For example, an NBA superstar who is exceptional in playing the sport may not have the skills required to be a coach or owner of a team. The organizational skills, leadership talents, and motivational tools used for his success as a player may not be effective for a team of players. When this occurs, the difficulties faced in the new role can consume resources in trying to resolve problems. Ultimately, this detracts from efforts in other areas where original successes occurred.

For the high achiever, buying into the assumption of global competence stems in part from a belief that he or she needs to be everything to everybody. Often, successful individuals fear they will miss out on an opportunity for even greater success or that the achievements they have already attained will be short-lived and transient. The truth is that you will inevitably miss out on some things because no one has unlimited resources and abilities to excel in every task demanded of them. The key is to choose which activities should be avoided and which ones are important to your key objectives toward success.

For those who demand greater responsibility of a high achiever, there is another false belief that accompanies that of global competence: a distorted view of exchange. By the law of reciprocity, when someone gives you something or does a favor for you, the expectation is that you will give or do something in return. For example, if a neighbor mows your lawn while you are away on vacation, he might expect you will do the same when he leaves town. However, the law of reciprocity becomes distorted when the one doing the favor is highly successful. The recipient in this situation does not feel the need to necessarily return the favor because the high achiever is in a favored position of status.

These assumptions and beliefs about the abilities of successful individuals and their duties to others place pressures on high achievers to take on more than they should. When this occurs, the ability to focus on important tasks becomes difficult because you spread yourself too thin. Understanding this is critical in determining exactly which tasks should be acted on and which roles should be fulfilled. If you try to be everything to everybody, you will soon realize that this way of thinking is not only detrimental to continued success but it is also impossible.

ATTENTION IS A LIMITED RESOURCE

Imagine for a moment someone with a diagnosis of attention deficit disorder (ADD). For individuals with severe ADD, focusing on a task or activity is incredibly difficult if not impossible for an extended length of time. The slightest noise or competing stimulation for attention throws their focus off track, and often they must start over on the task they were trying to complete. Thus, one of the behavioral treatments for ADD is to eliminate as many distractions as possible in order to allow for one's maximum attention. For sufferers of ADD, attention is a scarce commodity that must be nurtured and utilized in a precise way so daily tasks may be accomplished.

While you may not suffer from ADD, you also have a limited amount of attention and ability to focus—everyone does. If you sit in a quiet room alone and attempt to read a book, you likely will have little difficulty comprehending the story. But if you try to read the same passages while talking on the phone, watching television, and checking your email simultaneously, you will need to read it several times before the message sinks in. The rationale is the same behind recent state laws that forbid texting while driving. We each only have so much attention we can give at any one time. The more distractions that exist, the more demands we experience on our attention. And with less focused attention, we struggle to attain the high levels of achievement we desire.

When we accept too many roles and responsibilities, we jump from task to task trying to keep up with demands. Because this level of distraction causes us to exceed our abilities, we begin to struggle in one of two ways: Either we begin to cut corners and take shortcuts in our responsibilities in order to keep up with our long list of tasks; or we begin to neglect some of our responsibilities and fail to keep certain commitments we have made to others. Rather than taking a proactive approach in determining the healthy boundaries and level of responsibility we can maintain, we instead react to building pressures while we become increasingly unfocused and overwhelmed. By the time we realize we have overextended ourselves, backing out of the roles we have accepted becomes difficult and likely to have negative repercussions.

Imagine you wanted to give away $1 million to help fight poverty in a sub-Saharan country in Africa. As you investigate your options, you determine that two viable choices exist. You could either give the entire amount to a charitable organization that invested in economic recovery programs in the country, or you could give each of the one million inhabitants of the country a single dollar. By giving every individual a dollar, you may be recognized throughout the country by name, but the effort would have little long-term impact toward your goal. However, the charitable organization could take the entire amount and create programs that benefit the entire community for years to come. Which one seems more reasonable?

Similarly, when we allow distractions to overwhelm us because we take on too many responsibilities, our efforts become progressively diluted. With each new role, we have a little less attention and energy to give to the task. Instead of investing sizable amounts of our focus into select specific endeavors, we provide just enough effort to meet the minimum requirements of a wide variety of efforts, thereby resulting in diminished long-term effects.

Just like the donated $1 million, our attention must be invested wisely and appropriately. The goal is to achieve high-quality results in areas that best promote success rather than continually dilute our efforts. It is about quality, not quantity. The objective is to eliminate distractions so you can award enough attention to a task to achieve valuable, high-level results. Of course, this requires you to identify which roles are important and pertinent to your achievement goals. And as you travel along your journey of success, these goals may certainly change. Therefore, reassessing where you are and where you wish to go helps determine which responsibilities are ideal for you.

Every choice you make has a cost. The term for these lost chances are called "opportunity costs." We must understand not only what we are choosing in life but also what we are losing out on as we experience opportunity costs . I have learned this firsthand. As a recognized expert on the management of success, and someone who speaks around the country regularly, the number of invitations I've received from a variety of groups has increased over the years. Even early in my career, I was frequently asked to give free presentations for community groups, local organizations, and even my church. But I soon found that I was spreading my abilities too thin. I neglected to appreciate the opportunity costs associated with each speaking engagement I took. I lacked time to schedule national speaking engagements, enhance my talks and lectures, and develop more comprehensive educational programs. All of these things were important to me as achievement objectives, but I had failed to make them a priority over other responsibilities I had chosen. In other words, I had been distracted by lower priority tasks at the expense of my real needs to drive future success.

Sharing your success and abilities with family, friends, and your community is certainly worthwhile, and I regularly participate in such activities. However, I have learned that boundaries must be established so that such responsibilities are kept in proper perspective. The same applies to the barrage of communications we receive in today's world. The number of emails, texts, tweets, and other forms of communication can greatly distract our attention away from more important activities. Why do you think some celebrities and high-profile individuals hire professionals to manage their personal communications and screen their messages?

Distractions are the opponents to productivity. Essential activities and responsibilities that lead to continued success should top the list of priorities and receive our primary focus and attention. This means taking an inventory of what leads to success and what does not. Once these core responsibilities are secured and being performed with superior quality, other roles may be undertaken. But such additional duties should never demand so much of your attention that you begin making concessions in core areas. Ongoing assessment is required to determine if your focus is guiding you in the most effective direction. If done well, the likelihood you will continue along a path of high achievement is much greater.

TOOLS TO HELP YOU FOCUS

If you wish to stay on target, developing the ability to focus your attention on the roles and responsibilities most important to your success is important. Business owners realize that, in order to maintain their company's success, certain routine tasks, such as accounting, marketing, and the delivery of products and services, must be prioritized and

> The first step in refining your focus is to identify the basic responsibilities required for continued success.

routinely performed every day. Being distracted by outside responsibilities or tasks that hinder consistent performance of these core activities is a recipe for disaster.

Therefore, the first step in refining your focus is to identify the basic responsibilities required for continued success. For a professional baseball player, this may involve daily batting practice and weight-strengthening programs. For someone in a cutting edge industry such as digital entrepreneurship, this may involve an hour spent studying market trends and reading industry reports. A graduate student may require several hours of focused reading every day. Depending on the type of accomplishments you seek, a core set of responsibilities can be determined that will most efficiently help you achieve your goals. If you fail to define these essential tasks, then you risk being distracted by other, nonessential demands. Only you can determine what is most important for your success, and, therefore, you must continually examine where would be the best investment for your attention.

Once your core responsibilities have been defined, you next need to invoke some measure of priority management. Many successful individuals have a set routine and schedule that allows them to attend to the most important priorities regularly. Knowing that any distraction to these areas could prevent future success, additional responsibilities are avoided until these essential tasks have been performed. Of course, routine and schedules aren't much fun compared to spontaneity, but spontaneity invites distractions. There is nothing wrong with spontaneity, and, in fact, it promotes creativity and innovation. But being carefree at the expense of your priorities can cause you to award too little attention to high-achievement essentials. There's nothing wrong with a little dessert as long as it is part of an overall healthy diet.

Having defined priorities and success-related factors worthy of your attention, defining potential distractions is also worthwhile. Oftentimes, distractions are disguised. For example, being asked to participate on the board of an organization in your industry may seem like an opportunity to receive notoriety and showcase your talents, but it might also be a distraction from other tasks that need to be completed. For every opportunity and request of your time, an assessment of the opportunity costs should be made to determine if it is indeed a chance to further your success or a potential deterrent to your objectives. In this way, distractions can not only be defined but anticipated, allowing you to discern exactly which responsibilities and roles you are willing to take on.

The ability to define both valid opportunities and distractions is what creates boundaries, those limits within which you can function without overextending yourself. Perhaps the most difficult part of establishing boundaries is learning to say no, as previously discussed in the chapter titled "Limit the Love." Overcoming the desire to meet the expectations of others and the fear of missing out on some unique opportunity can be difficult. But if your goal is to pursue great accomplishments in your life, then you must become comfortable with refusing some demands.

Remember the discussion of global competence earlier? Awarding yourself a reality check about your true abilities can help you see your own limitations and justify turning down some requests. In other instances, being upfront and honest

> You cannot control how others react—you can only control how you respond.

about your inability to take on additional responsibilities gives you the satisfaction of being true to yourself and real to those around you. That may not mean your refusal will be well received, but you won't have to manage made-up excuses or avoid communications with those making the requests. Remember, you cannot control how others react—you can only control how you respond. Being honest about the boundaries you have established for your own personal goals provides the most direct and effective way in avoiding distractions.

THE IMPORTANCE OF GATEKEEPERS

Of course, saying no to every demand and explaining your boundaries repeatedly can become a distraction in and of itself. The time and attention awarded to politely declining opportunities and requests can also detract from your focus toward important priorities. Some successful individuals develop a type of filtering mechanism to screen important requests from unimportant ones. This could be something simple, such as automatic cataloging of subject-specific emails to various priority folders, or it may consist of something more elaborate, such as an electronic request form that must be filled out in detail. But for most, a gatekeeper—a designated individual who helps to buffer the barrage of requests and demands—is often employed as an ideal filtering method.

Gatekeepers may come from a variety of different sources. They may be family members who understand your priorities, or they may be someone whom you employ. For example, a financial manager may be an ideal gatekeeper if requests are constantly involving monetary requests for donations, investments, or support. Administrative assistants can screen calls, letters, and emails to identify which communications need your attention and which ones do not.

No matter who is selected as a gatekeeper, the most important thing is for them to understand your core responsibilities, your priorities, and the most common distractions in your life. If you can communicate these regularly to a gatekeeper, the utilization of this type of filter will help you focus your energies more effectively on the important tasks at hand.

MAINTAINING PROPER ALIGNMENT

For every moment of distraction, you lose valuable time out of your day. Likewise, the more distractions present, the less focus you have in any single activity. Unfortunately, as you travel along the road of success, high achievements progressively invite increasing demands for your attention. New opportunities present themselves, illusions of global competence develop, fears of disappointing others manifest, and expectations continually rise. Without a proactive ability to identify which responsibilities are important and which are distractions, the prospect of reaching higher levels of success becomes increasingly difficult. Instead, we react to every request at the expense of our own priorities.

Using the tools in this chapter, establishing boundaries, and defining success-related priorities lie at the heart of adopting a healthy attitude toward continued high achievement. This enables you to align your activities and responsibilities with your most important objectives while minimizing distractions and noise. Because attention is indeed a limited resource, you must safeguard it no differently than you would any other valuable commodity. By investing attention in the areas associated with continued success, your chances of enjoying a long life of great accomplishments becomes much more likely.

SUMMARY

The higher you rise, the more in demand you will be. You will not only have to deal with your own expectations regarding success but also the expectations of others. The confidence and competence you've gained through your journey can seduce you into thinking it is your duty to be the "end-all and be-all." Remember, just because you can do something, doesn't mean you should. The failure to maintain your focus will lead you into derailment, disappointment, and despair.

STRATEGIES

1. Define and prioritize the core elements of what it takes for continued success at your current position.
2. Develop routines and rituals that support the core elements.
3. Stop chasing the shiny objects that serve to keep you seeking when you should be creating.
4. Enroll others to help you stay on track.

SKILL #6:
DEALING WITH DOUBT

HOW TO NEUTRALIZE YOUR WORST CRITIC

> "I seek strength, not to be greater than other, but
> to fight my greatest enemy, the doubts within
> myself"
>
> –P.C. CAST, AUTHOR

The road to high achievement is plagued with doubts. From the time we begin to exert our independence as toddlers throughout our adult life, we inherently have concerns about whether we can accomplish the things we consider; we have doubt. Doubt is not all bad; a gnawing feeling of doubt can serve as a safeguard by preventing us from investing in endeavors unlikely to be successful. Doubt can also be used as a motivational mechanism and in effect becomes a means to promote self-confidence. These positive uses of doubt, however, must be separated from the negative effects of doubt, when it undermines our trust, self-esteem, and assertiveness.

Because doubt is a constant companion, understanding self-doubts and your reaction to others' doubts plays an important role in establishing healthy behaviors for success. Here I want to help you gain an appreciation for how doubt influences everyday behaviors and guides our decisions—sometimes this doubt is a healthy uncertainty that fosters wise choices, while other times it can lead to stagnation and ineffectiveness. By dealing with doubt in a constructive and positive way, you can ensure your continued efforts toward high achievement. Finding this balance is what truly defines the benefit of the doubt.

A PSYCHOLOGICAL PERSPECTIVE OF DOUBT

What is the origin of doubt? According to the psychologist Erik Erikson, toddlers first experience doubt as they begin to make their own independent choices. Between the ages of eighteen months and three years, children typically learn to use the toilet on their own, establish preferences about food and clothes, and select the types of toys they enjoy the most. Children who receive the proper support during this developmental stage are believed to be more secure and confident in their abilities. But for toddlers who struggle, due to a lack of support or other reasons, self-doubt and feelings of inadequacy become more likely. Therefore, the degree to which we experience doubt in our lives may partially reflect experiences that began very early in our human development.

Thus doubt represents the opposite of confidence. But having doubt does not mean you lack confidence altogether. Everyone has some degree of doubt because some feelings of uncertainty provide protections for our behaviors. For example, if I had no doubts whatsoever about my ability to predict the rise and fall of various financial stocks, I would recklessly invest monies in any stock I thought might be a winner. Only after losing my shirt would I realize my predictive abilities are lacking, but by then it could be too late.

According to Erikson, the realization of our weaknesses as well as strengths begins to develop at a very early age. Unfortunately, not all of us gain a healthy balance between confidence and doubt in childhood. Some of us have had parents who have, consciously or unconsciously, rendered undue criticisms of our efforts as children. As a result, parental doubt fosters our own self-doubts by shaming us at the expense of self-confidence. If these negative assessments continue, doubt evolves into a significant factor in our lives. Although many may succumb to such doubts and never try to accomplish high degrees of success in life, others use doubt as motivation toward high achievement. Among high achievers, doubt as a motivational force for success is actually quite common.

Numerous stories exist regarding individuals who have overcome adversity to reach the heights of success. Jim Carey, Oprah Winfrey, and J. K. Rowling are just a few celebrities who suffered difficult childhoods but persevered to attain amazing feats. For certain overachievers, proving wrong those who doubted their abilities can become the motivator; these individuals react to doubt with resilience and defiance. They work an excessive amount to overcome what they perceive as their inadequacies and shortcomings. As a result, these overachievers invest a surplus amount of energy and time into activities in order to make sure their goals are reached—and they actually end up going well beyond what is actually required. Though some may attain success, using doubt as motivation causes inefficiencies in their journey and allows their real objectives for life's accomplishments to be misplaced.

Although defiance and relentless overachieving can drive behaviors toward success, using excessive self-doubt of your abilities in this way can also become a distraction no different than taking on too many responsibilities, as discussed in the preceding chapter. Success is difficult to attain and even harder to maintain, and investing too much attention and energy into one area will always detract from others.

Much of what we have discussed under the psychology of doubt has addressed issues of self-doubt and self-confidence. But internal doubts represent only one aspect of the doubt successful individuals deal with. Both during your ascent and after you have reached high levels of achievement, doubts from others within your environment will also have a significant effect on your thoughts, feelings, and decisions. How you feel about your own abilities can all too easily be influenced by the doubts of others. Therefore, you must also have a good understanding of why others may doubt you and their underlying reasons for expressing such uncertainties. Like self-doubt, a degree of criticism from others can be constructive, but awarding too much value to external doubts can be detrimental.

SELF-DOUBT VERSUS OTHERS' DOUBT

Although you may have many proponents in your corner as well as tremendous support to reach a high level of achievement, you likely recognize that there can be just as many or more naysayers and doubters among the crowd reminding you of the difficulties involved, the odds against you, and the many who have failed before you. Keeping a positive outlook and a realistic perspective is important in these situations. If not, you may let the doubts of others either keep you from pursuing the goals you desire or else

> There can be just as many or more naysayers and doubters among the crowd reminding you of the difficulties involved, the odds against you, and the many who have failed before you.

replace your healthy motivation to succeed with a draining need to prove others wrong.

Why does it seem so common for others to doubt our abilities for high achievement and our chances for success? Do our accomplishments negatively affect them in some way that makes them root against us? The answers to these questions are somewhat complicated. The most common reason others express uncertainty about our potential for success involves their own self-doubts. When individuals have strong self-doubts about their own skills and talents, they often project those perceptions onto others around them. Therefore, when someone doubts our chances, it may simply be a reflection of the thoughts they have about their own possibilities for high achievement.

In addition to the projection of self-doubt onto others and expressions of poor trust, people also have a natural tendency to focus on the negative side of things. This is a protective stance—people naturally want to be correct in their predictions and beliefs. When they must face being wrong, their self-confidence and self-esteem can be hurt. Therefore, taking the negative side of things is a natural way of hedging one's bets.

You only need to listen to your local sports talk radio show to hear how such doubt plays out in a fan's psyche. Fans often call before an upcoming match to express their doubts about their team's performance. They often focus entirely on the weaknesses of their team and the strengths of the opponent. You can hear the anxiousness in their voices, and the radio program itself serves as some type of reassurance and therapy for their uncertainty and doubt. The reason that these callers doubt from the start is because it provides a matter of self-protection. If they somehow foresee their team's demise, they can at least be comforted in the fact that they were knowledgeable enough to see it coming. In other words, they throw their team partially under the bus in order to preserve their own self-confidence.

For individuals who lack a great deal of confidence and self-esteem, criticizing high achievers and their accomplishments helps them level the playing field in a similar way. They tear others down so they may feel more valuable themselves. For example, a film celebrity who has received numerous awards may be criticized for his or her inability to keep a stable relationship, for his or her lack of appreciation of fans, or for a false perception of talent. These negative traits attempt to diminish the actor's achievements. The critic feels empowered by comparison because they believe they excel in these areas where the actor is failing. Belittling and doubting others' talents is thus a means to enhance our own sense of self-worth.

Finally, the need for attention causes other individuals to express doubts and uncertainties about our chances for success. Seeking attention through doubting is a way to be heard and feel empowered. If I cannot be successful on my own merits, critiquing others allows me to be acknowledged in relation to someone else's achievements. The vocal expression of doubt is therefore a chance to ride someone else's coattails and receive recognition in the process. By announcing uncertainty in someone else's ability, the person creates an antagonistic and sometimes controversial platform from which they can be heard.

When doubt is used in this context, it emanates from feelings of jealousy and envy. By understanding this, you can realize such doubts are actually a form of admiration. Rather than allowing the doubts of others to affect your own confidence and trust in your abilities, you can recognize them as distorted expressions of flattery. If you hadn't attained some level of achievement for which public attention was being awarded, the individuals criticizing would have no need to doubt your abilities. It is only because you have attained success that their doubts have some type of power and benefit for them. Turning this perception around can help you continue to focus on healthy objectives rather than succumbing to negativity.

Perhaps the most powerful form of such doubt comes through the media. If you look closely at a sampling of news items and stories, comparatively few portray positive perceptions and outcomes. We hear or read the headlines about someone being accused of a crime for several days in a row; if they are exonerated, however, the story is typically buried deep in the publication or program. Likewise, if a reputable person expresses their doubts about a sports team, a performer, or a corporate executive, that individual's opinions are frontline news compared to someone else singing that subject's praises. Negativity, controversy, and doubt get attention, and increased attention means greater media outreach. You will always hear voices of uncertainty long before you hear the voices of support.

Unfortunately, doubts presented in the public media are very powerful. In a culture immersed in 24/7 news and entertainment, public uncertainty is hard to escape. You must have a solid foundation of self-confidence and trust to weather such negative portrayals of yourself, and you must have a strong understanding of the motivations behind the doubters. While self-doubts can spur our own personal

> You will always hear voices of uncertainty long before you hear the voices of support.

development, external doubts are less likely to reflect realistic assessments of our abilities.

REACTING TO DOUBT

Doubt inherently creates a sense of fear within us. What if we fail? What if we can't attain our goals? The risks of embarrassment, criticism, humiliation, and more enter our thoughts as our uncertainty grows in strength. How we react to this fear determines to a great extent whether we pursue healthy behaviors or not. If we fear the repercussions of failure too strongly, we may become unwilling to take risks at all, thus making success impossible to achieve. Or, instead, our fears may push us toward perfectionism, as we believe we must be excessively confident in our abilities before pursuing an activity. In this sense, doubt can create paralysis. Unless we can recognize and define our fears in relation to feelings of uncertainty, we remain stuck in a state of stagnation, hoping the fear will miraculously subside.

The underlying issue when doubt-induced fear takes over is our lack of self-confidence. Either we have allowed self-doubt to diminish our faith in our own abilities, or we have let others' opinions convince us that we cannot succeed. We have lost trust that we can perform to the degree necessary to achieve our goals. We become progressively less likely to take risks. We become more untrusting of our skills and talents. Without positive feedback to help strengthen our faith in our abilities, our doubts remain in control of our actions. As a result, giving into our doubt becomes a self-fulfilling prophecy as we continually reinforce our belief that we cannot achieve success.

With increasing doubt, we may become less willing to accept feedback and criticism from others. Because such comments threaten our confidence and trust even further, we may choose to take an avoidant position. If we close our eyes and ears to negative feedback, we believe we will suffocate our doubts from gaining greater influence. But such a psychological defense hinders our ability to grow in the process. Without feedback or criticism, we lose the opportunity to hear healthy and constructive comments that could help us achieve even greater accomplishments. As we starve our doubts, we also starve our growth.

Not only can uncertainty induce a degree of paralysis toward future growth, it undermines accurate self-assessments. In the late 1970s, research was conducted on a group of women who had attained significant success. These investigations revealed a condition known as "impostor syndrome". Despite having achieved tremendous accomplishments, some of these women attributed their success to luck, good timing, or some other external influence. In essence, they felt like frauds, and they did not attribute their achievements to their own abilities. A void or emptiness resided within them, which they felt a need to cover up and hide from exposure. As a result, their self-doubts drove them to constantly achieve in hopes of preventing someone finding out they were actually impostors.

Though it was initially demonstrated among successful women, the impostor syndrome has been found in men and women alike. For individuals who suffer from this complex, uncertainty in their own abilities has become so strong that they cannot trust themselves. They also lack trust in others and fear confiding in others about their concerns. Their only recourse is thus to strive for complete perfection and to remain vigilant in hiding any part of their behavior that might be perceived as a weakness. This results in unhealthy motivations for success and a faulty foundation upon which to build future growth.

In some instances, those who feel like an impostor may be driven by doubt to achieve, but often when doubt is the driver, the ability to take healthy risks declines. This situation results in emotional extremes; individuals fluctuate from a need to overcome feelings of uncertainty to a total lack of trust in themselves and others. Because their confidence is poor, their strength to take risks becomes diminished. In order to continue to grow in our achievements, healthy risks must be taken. Discernment regarding risks is important, but such discernment comes from a foundation of trust and confidence in one's self and in others—not from a foundation of uncertainty.

When dealing with doubt it is best to consider some of the most common forms expressed by high achievers. These are the doubts of ability, acceptability, and sustainability.

DOUBTS OF ABILITY

As mentioned previously, doubts of ability refer to the questions "Can I really do this?" or "Do I have what it takes?" It doesn't matter what has been achieved in the past. When starting a new venture or being requested to do something different, this question can always lie underneath. Unaddressed, doubts of ability can lead to excessive worry and nervousness that diminish your capacity to complete the tasks at hand. It can also erode the confidence others have in you.

> "Can I really do this?" or "Do I have what it takes?"

In order to minimize these doubts, we begin by embracing

healthy doubt. Fighting doubt or pretending that it is not there can be exhausting. Embracing it as a natural part of the journey can free that psychological energy you have been wasting. Healthy doubt helps us pay closer attention and lays the groundwork for moving us forward. It serves to help us slow down and consider the best options before proceeding, and through that process we gain more confidence. Unhealthy doubt, on the other hand, tends to create paralysis and diminishes confidence. It threatens to keep us constantly second-guessing ourselves, thereby preventing the necessary progress forward.

As we counter doubts of ability, it is sometimes useful to change the questions. Tinges of doubt that appear as anxiety and nervousness can be mitigated by asking yourself questions that help redirect your focus and produce an empowered state. "Can I really do this?" forces the mind into judgment mode. It is not a type of question that leads to any traction. A labeling question such as, "What exactly do I fear or doubt?" helps to reduce ambiguity and provides some level of clarity and control. Confidence building questions such as, "What have I done before that was more challenging than this?" or "Who believes that I can do this?" direct the mind to look for supporting evidence to accomplish the task at hand. And finally, future-oriented questions such as, "How will I feel when this is accomplished?" or "What doors are going to be opened once I get through this?"—these types of questions can also create a positive state that help push one past the pain.

> Perfection is more of an idealized end product. It is static in nature, and it can be both confining and suffocating.

We can also focus on excellence, not perfection. The seduction and pressure to be perfect can be immense. It is easy to think that the outcome has to look and feel a certain way or else we have failed. The key here is to get out of black-or-white thinking mode. Differentiating excellence and perfection can be helpful. In essence, excellence is about doing something well. It's a dynamic process that leads to optimal results. Perfection is more of an idealized end product. It is static in nature, and it can be both confining and suffocating. Most often, perfectionism leads one into feeling perpetually "less than." Accepting that no matter where you are or how far you have come, we are all "works in progress." Remembering this can help thwart the tendencies to be overly self-critical.

Finally, we all must act in spite of doubt. Doubt is often disguised as a fear of the unknown. When this is the case the only way to alleviate doubt and the unknown is to proceed forward and find out

> Doubt is often disguised as a fear of the unknown.

what you need to know. This is why one of my most repeated sayings is "motion breeds clarity." As you proceed forward, you inevitably gain the information and awareness of what needs to happen next. This, in turn, leads to greater degrees of confidence.

DOUBTS OF ACCEPTABILITY

Doubts that relate to acceptance are common to those whose achievements have led them into different social circles and environments. For example, many students from all backgrounds who are matriculating at elite colleges or graduate programs will quietly ask themselves the question "Do I belong?" When this form of doubt prevails you may feel compelled to spend your focus on "fitting in" rather than "figuring out" what it takes to succeed performance-wise. In order to stay on track, consider that you belong because you are there; you earned it. Everyone has a journey that is specific to him or her. Everyone has unique challenges to overcome and opportunities that they had to take advantage of to succeed. Your journey is neither greater nor lesser than anyone else's so don't spend time in trying to convince yourself that you are not worthy. Worthiness is a state of mind.

It also helps to stay connected to your "why." Connect with the reasons that you have achieved your objective, the importance of whom you are serving, whether it is your clients, family, or community. These are the people you are succeeding for, in addition to yourself. Thinking of them will help you keep the big picture in mind.

> "Self-acceptance is the first level of acceptance we all need because placing our self-worth in the hands of others is a treacherous game that will always leave us short-changed."

Finally, remember that validation is an inside game. Constantly searching for acceptance can be a covert way of seeking validation, but we know that we can't please everyone and not everyone will accept us. Self-acceptance is the first level of acceptance we all need because placing our self-worth in the hands of others is a treacherous game that will always leave us short-changed.

DOUBTS OF SUSTAINABILITY

Outstanding performances on the field, in the classroom, and in sales set a standard in your mind and the minds of others as a high achiever. After the initial hype dies down, the question of "Can I keep this up, or can I do it again?"

surfaces. I have witnessed individuals go to great lengths to sabotage their further efforts in order to lower expectations. Despite knowing that they have the capacity to do well, often the fear of "having" to play all out and constantly exceed expectations causes them to feel exhausted at the very thought. It then becomes easier to play small in order to avoid disappointment.

In order to counter the doubts related to sustainability you need to first manage your energy. This entails increasing both physical and mental stamina. The more you find ways to increase your capacity to deal with the pressures and pitfalls, the easier it will be to meet the next challenge. Additionally, energy conservation can be a result of learning to master the three Ds, i.e., learning the difference between what you should do, what you should delegate, and what you should delete.

Every journey has several ups and downs. What we need to focus on is consistent growth, and that means avoiding intense attachments to either the highs or the lows, because both are temporary. A growth focus frees you to push the envelope rather than getting stuck in the past. It also allows you to position your strengths. There is nothing more exhausting than trying to be someone you are not or trying to do something that is outside of your gifts. You may be able to pretend for a while, but eventually the façade fades. Sustainability will be based on your ability to lean on your natural know-how and outsource the rest.

> A growth focus frees you to push the envelope rather than getting stuck in the past.

Finally, as with many of the challenges in this book, the

doubt of sustainability is often best countered by outside support. Being willing and able to openly to talk about your trials and challenges helps to alleviate the psychological load often experienced by the high achiever. Whether it be a mentor, colleague, or family member, doubt can be easily overcome when you operate from the knowledge that you have a strong, supportive network.

POSITIVE WAYS TO DEAL WITH DOUBT

So how do we deal with doubt if it is an ever-present companion on our journey toward success? Eliminating all occasions of doubt is impossible and would likely result in very hollow victories along the way. Therefore, we must develop healthy ways to incorporate uncertainties into our achievement behaviors and growth mindset. Unhealthy reactions to doubt can cause serious problems in attaining and maintaining success over time, but normalizing some degree of doubt fosters better discernment and continued personal growth.

In most cases, social support goes a long way toward adopting healthy strategies, and effective strategies in dealing with doubt are no different. We all have some healthy relationships in our lives, those in which we have strong trust and confidence. Doubt is only a very minor player in these dynamics. Instead, these relationships provide important insights for us and help us establish new areas of competency moving forward. Why do we have such great trust and such little doubt in some of our existing relationships? Is it a certain attribute these people have, or is it simply the fact we have had the benefit of getting to know them over a long length of time? Identifying the key ingredients that foster trust and minimize doubt is useful in helping us develop new and healthy relations.

For most people, time is the most common ingredient for reducing doubt and building trust. But time is not always a luxury we have. Many successful individuals are thrust into immediate relationships with agents, financial planners, and teammates. With such limited time, it becomes difficult to ever gain a high level of trust if time is the only qualifier. In these situations, the use of other forms of social proof may be helpful. Referrals, testimonials, and endorsements from others we already trust can provide us with a sense of security and certainty in instances where we don't have the ability to "get to know" someone. This substitute enables us to still approach new relationships with a healthy degree of doubt but not to the point that it hinders our growth.

The key to reducing doubt in a logical way comes through building confidence in our decision-making abilities. We achieve this through small successes, which lead to greater knowledge and awareness. Each occasion for mastering our doubts or dispelling the doubts of others is a victorious battle in what can feel like a very long war.

Doubt is such a formidable opponent because what underlies doubt is fear. We fear we may be mistreated or lose something dear to us. We fear others may be seeking their own benefit at our expense. Fears are as numerous as doubts, and identifying the fear behind the doubt is important. Because fear can be either helpful or restrictive, understanding fear is a must if we want to assess whether it is rational or not. Some fears are completely supported and serve to help us take appropriate precautions, but others are irrational and become restrictive of our progress.

Neither doubt nor fear is necessarily a bad thing. In fact, neither of them is good or bad. Taking doubt out of this moral realm is important for a healthy perspective to develop.

Instead, doubt and uncertainty should be viewed as effective or ineffective, constructive or restrictive, growth-promoting or growth-prohibitive. If we can detach moral connotations from our fears and doubts, we can then examine doubt based on outcomes. Did this doubt protect me from harm, or did it hinder my ability to achieve? By accepting our doubt as a natural ingredient to success, we come to utilize doubt more effectively and rationally as a guide to our behaviors. Ultimately, this allows us to continue on a path toward higher achievement without becoming paralyzed by irrational, emotionally based fears.

DOUBT IS OUR TOOL FOR SUCCESS

Unfortunately, doubt has been given a bad name. People who doubt their abilities are often described as lacking confidence or self-esteem. Individuals who doubt others' abilities or motives are labeled as paranoid or suspicious. But doubt is a normal part of our design. It is there for a reason. Without doubt, we may never consider possible negative outcomes that could seriously hinder our future successes. Doubt is not only helpful in this light but absolutely necessary. Without doubt, we simply become reckless and potentially destructive. But by listening to our inner voice of uncertainty, we can better process logically whether or not our next move should be taken or not.

Like any tool, doubt can be used effectively or ineffectively. In order for it to serve us best, we must understand our own personal doubts and the rationale behind them. Only then can we make intelligent choices about whether our doubt is being used to our ultimate benefit or not.

SUMMARY

The road to high achievement is plagued with doubts. Healthy doubt can serve as a source of motivation and protection. Unhealthy doubt can lead to excessive worry and self-handicapping behaviors. Three common forms of doubt that high achievers face are: doubts of ability, doubts of acceptability, and doubts of sustainability. Regardless of what you accomplish, doubt will be a constant companion that must be appropriately embraced or confronted in order to free up the psychological energy needed for sustainable results.

INSIGHTS AND STRATEGIES

1. Embrace healthy doubt and use it as a competitive edge.
2. Focus on excellence rather than perfection.
3. Act in spite of doubt. Motion breeds clarity and confidence.
4. Connect with a support system that guides you and helps remind you of what you are capable.

SKILL #7:
GRIEVE AND GROW

HOW TO COPE WITH WHAT YOU LOSE WHEN YOU SUCCEED

> "The truth is, unless you let go, unless you for-
> give yourself, unless you forgive the situation,
> unless you realize that the situation is over, you
> cannot move forward."
>
> —STEVE MARABOLI,
> AUTHOR OF UNAPOLOGETICALLY YOU:
> REFLECTIONS ON LIFE AND THE HUMAN EXPERIENCE

Grieving is a part of life. Whether we have lost a loved one, said good-bye to a job, or moved on from a relationship, whenever we part with something we cherish, we must regularly deal with disappointment. Interestingly, few realize that the road toward success is filled with such losses. When we transition from one step to the next, those transitions involve letting go of our past and embracing an uncertain future. We experience a natural tendency to cling to the things we find familiar and comforting, but in order to continue our journey and our growth, we must learn to grieve our losses. Other disappointments occur on the road to success as well; sometimes they are based on the expectations we have of ourselves, and other times they are based on our expectations of others. One thing is for certain: Disappointments are bound to occur as we attain greater levels of success, and learning how to deal with them well is immensely helpful.

With the seventh skill, you will come to appreciate the common disappointments experienced by successful individuals and the transitions that must be made in order to continue along a path of increasing success. Failure to let go and grieve effectively can result in a number of negative consequences that may hinder future growth and progress. By shedding light on these consequences and through the adoption of healthy behaviors, these pitfalls can be avoided. Disappointments are inevitable, but they do not have to be your downfall. Accepting them and learning from them can actually provide a wonderful means by which continued risks and growth can effectively evolve.

THE DISAPPOINTMENTS OF SUCCESS

Dealing with disappointments may be one of the biggest challenges for successful individuals. It starts as a kind of paradox—after all, if you're successful, you're not supposed to be disappointed, right? Unfortunately nothing could be further from the truth. Think about the first time you experienced some major achievement in your life. Perhaps it was making the honor roll in school or scoring the winning goal for your sports team. What likely happened afterward was a changed perspective regarding your abilities. Higher levels of achievement bring about changes impossible to predict. From an internal perspective, your needs change as you attain greater success. Though you may feel very comfortable with the behaviors that got you to where you are, different behaviors will be needed to experience continued personal growth. Clinging to old ways of doing things and old relationships can create barriers. In addition, greater success causes others to increase their expectations of you. Meeting these expectations may or may not be realistic, and distinguishing between healthy expectations and unhealthy ones is important. In both instances, you will have to deal with disappointments whether they come from the loss of old comforts or the failure to meet others' expectations.

As achievements become more significant, the potential for the losses of disappointment to mount becomes more intense. Consider for example some of the latest winners on American Idol. They start out as small-town singers with little fame, and suddenly they are catapulted to instant national renown and recognition. They can no longer go back to the familiar environment they knew prior to their fame. Their ability to enjoy privacy has shrunk dramatically overnight, and the time to invest in past relationships is suddenly compromised by new relationships that involve their new career. In aspiring to high achievements, these losses are rarely anticipated; when they occur unexpectedly, the time (and space) to appreciate such disappointments is limited.

> Higher levels of achievement bring about changes impossible to predict.

Because change and transition are unavoidable as one reaches higher levels of accomplishment, disappointments are an inevitable component of this journey. Change is a constant—in this case it is dictated by the new situation and forced upon you. You then essentially have two basic choices: You can accept the change and make the appropriate transition, or you can resist and struggle to balance between your past and present. If you choose the latter, problems ensue because no one can be in two places at once. Ultimately, you may lose the opportunity to attain greater success as a result of this choice. If the disappointments are acknowledged and dealt with in a healthy fashion, however, then progressive levels of achievement can be enjoyed.

In his book Managing Transitions, William Bridges views change and transition as different entities. Unlike change, which is purely situational, transitions are psychological in nature. Bridges describes three phases

> Unless one can let go and accept losses, growth cannot proceed.

for every transition: an ending, a neutral zone, and a new beginning. During the ending phase, individuals making healthy transitions not only recognize the losses present but likewise appreciate the opportunities ahead. The process of letting go of the past—both what happened and what didn't happen—and accepting the possibilities of the future is the most difficult of the three phases. It is also the most important. Unless one can let go and accept losses, growth cannot proceed.

The next phase, the neutral zone, represents a stage disconnected from the past but yet not fully engaged in the present. In this stage of transition, reorientation is required so the new beginning can proceed. Though this stage may feel unproductive, internal and external adjustments are being made to allow one to deal with the disappointments and losses of the past while simultaneously adopting a new perspective. Once this reorientation occurs, a new beginning is able to proceed as new priorities are established. The transition is eventually completed as the change is fully accepted by not only yourself but also by others around you.

CHALLENGES IN DEALING WITH DISAPPOINTMENTS

Once you have acknowledged that with success naturally come disappointments then adopting effective coping methods to further advance your growth can become less difficult. But make no mistake, there will be several potential challenges along the way. Among the most common is a failure to let go. Attachments to the things that led to your initial achievements are hard to relinquish. A degree of security resides within these proven behaviors, relations, and beliefs. But future success requires constant adaptation; unless you are willing to let go and move forward, you can become stagnant or even regress.

Another subtle yet powerful challenge that occurs with increasing levels of achievement is the need for relationships to change. Not all of them, of course, and not all in the same way, but many existing dynamics need to shift in order to facilitate positive growth. Family relationships are a good example. Despite your significant success, certain family members may continue to perceive you in an outdated manner, which limits your abilities to expand. This is very similar to the experience of an addict who is now clean. He or she has to deal with the fact that family and acquaintances may still see and treat him or her as an addict. These types of fixated perceptions are naturally based on interactions over many years. However, these perceptions only have this power if you allow them to have it. Forcing yourself to play small despite your growth in order to appease the limiting expectations of some family members or friends is an example of how the failure to let go can be detrimental.

Some relations need to change as we reach higher levels of achievement and some actually must end. This is simply a natural progression that occurs as individuals grow in different directions. How many of your old high school buddies do you still keep in contact with on a regular basis? In all likelihood, the number is small; the ones you do still communicate with probably have traveled a similar path of success as yourself. At the very least, both of you have allowed the relationship to change along the way. As people progress in life, relationships naturally change. This does not mean we cannot grieve the loss of the way things were, but we must accept the changes at some point if we wish to continue to grow.

One of the unforeseen challenges of success is the speed with which certain changes occur; we lack the time to adjust to different ways of relating and to grieve lost relationships. Without time for mental transitions to occur, we risk becoming stuck in a stage of grief, which can hinder our future abilities. For some, the grieving process can be quite prolonged simply because our ability to focus on the process at the outset is so limited.

The five classic stages of grief are: denial, anger, bargaining, depression, and, ultimately, acceptance. What many fail to realize is that acceptance is not a given outcome of this process. Whether grieving the death of a loved one or the loss of familiar environments due to sustained success, individuals can become stuck in any one of these stages. Denial is common when time is limited because our ability to process the loss is constrained. In an effort to avoid shock or other sad emotions, denial is used as a buffer. If the loss is never dealt with effectively, isolation or resentment may develop as pain becomes redirected as anger. We may even develop resentment toward our own success.

In order to transition well, we must have time to realize the losses and disappointments of a new status and deal with them effectively. If that time is not immediately available, then time should be reserved later to allow grief and transition to occur more completely. Time may not be the only limitation—for some, adequate support may be the problem. Consider the business employee who is suddenly promoted to a managerial position. Overnight, the person's relationships with his fellow employees have changed from that of a coworker to a supervisor. The source of his prior camaraderie and comfort may now be gone as well if it resided among his peers. Many times when such changes occur, people lack a place to work through their disappointments. This is what I mean by resources: The old habits that provided support are no longer available, and new ones have yet to be established.

Other struggles appear in dealing with transitions. For example, during their initial road to success many people become reliant on positive feedback and compliments to boost their energy and efforts. But as higher levels of achievement occur, expectations increase and criticisms from others are more common. This increase in negative commentary can undermine your behaviors, particularly if you have come to rely on encouragement as your motivation. Unless this is anticipated as a natural part of greater success, negative reactions such as depression, avoidance, isolation, and an aversion to risk-taking can all develop as a result.

Similarly, the stress of a new environment can affect individuals who hail from a very different place of origin. When under stress we often revert back to behaviors learned in childhood. Take, for example, the athlete who grew up in an underserved urban environment. Outside of the work that went into becoming skillful in his sport, he has also had to develop social skills adequate for survival in this particular community. In his new professional world he will have to resist the urge to address confrontation in the manner that worked in his prior culture, because such behaviors are not likely to be effective in their new environment. Unless they can adopt new behaviors and strategies in line with their new priorities, they will likely fail. All of us are similarly prone to regression under stress rather than through growth and change. As a result, our transitions become ineffective.

Perhaps the most detrimental reaction to the stress of change is a condition known as learned helplessness. Originally identified in animals, the exposure to repeated aversive stimulation without an ability to escape eventually leads to general inaction despite the level of pain experienced. This level of helplessness and inaction can occur in people who are constantly subjected to negative feedback. In this situation, individuals begin to feel they lack control of their environment. They quit seeking ways to change or adapt because nothing they seem to do makes a difference. They develop an inability to see new opportunities as they continue to focus only on the negative aspects of their current situation and their inability to change it. Unfortunately, this becomes a self-fulfilling prophecy that leads to isolation and stagnation, which leads people to avoid receiving feedback. Because they feel their risk of failure is ever-increasing, they resign themselves to either quit trying or to ignore any and all feedback. Learned helplessness thus results in depression and self-pity on the one hand, and resentment and irritability on the other. Because priorities have not been well defined, people become emotionally vulnerable to any failure.

For many who reach higher levels of accomplishment, natural barriers in effectively dealing with disappointments do exist. These include time constraints and a lack of support in understanding one's needs during a transition from one level to another. Allowing new priorities to develop along with new behaviors can be difficult especially when the old way of doing things feels more secure and comfortable.

THE COSTS OF LETTING LOSS AND DISAPPOINTMENTS GUIDE OUR BEHAVIORS

Rather than grieving in a healthy fashion and accepting the losses along the way, sometimes a poor transition can affect our day-to-day functioning. Our disappointments remain in the forefront, dictating how we behave instead of allowing for our desires and dreams to lead the way. For example, if we constantly feel guilty for changes in a close relationship, we may make poor choices when trying to maintain a closeness that is no longer practical. In other instances, failing to grieve effectively can even cause us to shut down completely in order to avoid further letdowns. These behaviors are just some of the detrimental consequences of allowing our disappointments to guide how we behave instead of the other way around, all of which lead to bigger problems down the road as they obstruct our future successes.

As you move up the ladder of success, increased demands and responsibilities will occur. Increased expectations based on past achievements will develop. But like everyone else, you only have twenty-four hours in a day, and you still have to manage your time efficiently. That means you will no longer be able to serve all the same roles you did previously. While others may not understand or even accept this change, you must realize and accept it in order to manage your accomplishments well. Once this happens, you become able to establish new boundaries and adopt newly defined roles that are well aligned with your new status. Unfortunately, many times our guilt and difficulty in letting go gets in the way.

As discussed in the chapter titled "Limit the Love," one of the most significant consequences of allowing disappointments to rule our actions is a failure to set boundaries. For some reason, we perceive boundaries in a negative light. If we tell a friend we can no longer meet for lunch every week, we fear they will take this the wrong way. By saying no, we feel we are somehow rejecting their friendship, or at least we fear they will perceive it that way. The same thing can happen to a more profound degree in relationships we need to end altogether. The finality of these boundary decisions affects us very deeply, and we feel the grief and guilt more intensely as a result.

Such feelings make us rethink things and reexamine our goals and dreams. It may be that these fears and emotions are serving as healthy measures for us to assess whether our pursuits align well with our values and vision. In such cases, changing our behavior is worthwhile. However, changing how we behave in order to simply avoid guilt and the pain of change without a corresponding reassessment of our goals takes us off the path of success and leads us down a different road. Stuck between an inability to let go and a desire to move ahead, we become frustrated and resentful as we fail to progress. For this reason, as higher levels of achievement are attained, establishing new boundaries for our relationships over time is essential for a healthy growth mindset.

In an attempt to be everything to everyone, we can lose focus and become short-sighted. Because we are most concerned about what we are losing, we fail to see what we might stand to gain. New and exciting opportunities are ignored because we are too busy trying to cope with guilt. The same applies to disappointments related to our failures. When we fail, we become consumed with our shortcomings and how we might be perceived now that we have failed. Instead, we should consider which things we did well and how we can learn from them. In other words, if we keep looking at the glass as half-empty by focusing on our disappointments, we will never quench our thirst with the glass that is half-full.

Other consequences from dealing poorly with disappointments involve how we internalize and react to their effects. In some cases, we may grow to dislike the feelings of disappointment so much that we choose strategies to avoid them at all costs. For example, failures can lead us to become excessively thorough by double- and triple-checking our every move. In essence, we have determined that making a mistake is simply intolerable. We invest surplus amounts of energy into ensuring such situations are never encountered again. But in the process, we limit our potential to achieve greater accomplishments because we exhaust our resources inefficiently. We are so overzealous in our efforts to avoid future disappointments we end up restricting our future level of success.

We may also choose to avoid disappointment by shying away from taking future risks. The chances of being disappointed are much less if we decide to only pursue things that are easy, safe, and certain. But by adopting such avoidance behavior, we can actually cause greater disappointments because making mistakes and taking risks are not only acceptable but a beneficial part of growth. Through our mistakes we learn new strategies, realize new solutions, and better understand our goals. Therefore, allowing ourselves to make mistakes and learning how to grieve any disappointments in a positive manner enables us to become stronger and wiser. With better insights and discernment, we can then adjust and adapt in a way that best serves us. But if we choose to avoid mistakes at all costs through excessive precautions or reduced risk-taking, we naturally constrain our personal progress.

At its worst, avoidance behavior leads to isolation as a result of our inability to grieve and accept disappointments. We may run from criticisms so we do not have to experience others' dissatisfaction. We become paralyzed as we quit taking chances. The pain of disappointment becomes so powerful we will do anything to escape it. And in the process, we find ourselves alone and unsatisfied. Ultimately, this can lead to depression, resentment, anger, and other negative emotions. Similar to someone who has lost a loved one, we may be unable to bear the pain of losing something close to us. While this may seem to protect us from further hurt, we sacrifice their chance for happiness and personal fulfillment in the process. As the adage goes, it is better to have loved and lost than to never have loved at all.

> Making mistakes and taking risks are not only acceptable but a beneficial part of growth.

EFFECTIVE MEASURES IN DEALING WITH DISAPPOINTMENT

Simply realizing that disappointments are a part of success can go a long way in helping you cope with loss and change. Rather than avoid the losses of transition, the more disappointments you experience, the more adept you will become in dealing with failures and dissatisfactions. Mistakes become perceived as positive tools through which greater growth and achievement can be attained, and transitioning

> Rather than avoid the losses of transition, the more disappointments you experience, the more adept you will become in dealing with failures and dissatisfactions.

becomes easier and easier as a result. In this spirit, some measures can be taken to assist you in this maturing process; by implementing them, you will place yourself in a better position to excel.

Establishing boundaries that align with your ever-changing responsibilities is important. But communicating these changes within existing relationships can be tough. Past friends and family members may expect things to stay the same even though your higher status and increased demands make this difficult, if not impossible. By seeing the bigger picture, you can understand that resources must be reallocated as you progress. This means redefining boundaries for both existing relationships and activities as well as new ones. Saying no is a necessary part of success because more and more people will want your attention as you excel. By acknowledging and accepting this change, you create healthy limits that foster future success.

Of course, feeling disappointed with losses, change, and failures is perfectly normal. The presence of disappointment is not the primary problem. Rather the real culprit is the ineffective way of handling disappointment by reacting out of guilt or an avoidance of hurt. In addition to acknowledging the

> The real culprit is the ineffective way of handling disappointment by reacting out of guilt or an avoidance of hurt.

presence of disappointment, securing time and a place to grieve is necessary. Often the demands of higher achievement limit these opportunities, but this pause lets you appreciate what is being lost. From there, you can learn to accept your new situation while realizing new opportunities for growth along the way. Even if the grieving process must be delayed, making time to reflect on how your life has changed provides positive insights that help you grow.

Being able to learn from past mistakes naturally empowers us to improve. Similarly, past relationships can be seen as necessary experiences in our lives that helped us to grow. Studying how our past has allowed us to reach the present level of achievement is important because success requires us to continue to improve the higher we climb. But unlike a map that has a clear starting point and destination, the road to success often has detours, roadblocks, unexpected turns—even the destination may change! Through your disappointments, you can better define who you are, as well as what you want to become. Rather than blindly reacting to every disappointment without deeper consideration, contemplation and reflection serve you best as part of your personal development.

Finally, nothing helps us more than having a mentor or someone who has already been there. A natural sense of sadness occurs when we become disappointed that things are not going as we wish. During these times, it helps to have support from someone

> Through your disappointments, you can better define who you are, as well as what you want to become.

who truly understands our situation. Finding these individuals may seem tough at times, especially as our time and mental space are constrained by our higher achievements. But if you can seek others who have experienced the same disappointments and failures as you have, their wisdom can provide healthy guidance and often prevent additional pain and difficulty.

No one ever said becoming successful was easy, and few people realize exactly what is involved when they begin to attain greater success in their lives. Relationships you thought would never change evaporate into thin air. Familiar situations, of which you have fond memories, no longer exist. And all the while, demands are increasing on your time and energy as expectations rise. Because of these realities, disappointments are indeed inevitable along the path to success. Acknowledging this fact and learning how to cope with transition becomes one of the most important skills you can develop to foster continued growth and fulfillment.

SUMMARY

The higher you rise, the more likely you are to experience significant losses and disappointments. As you journey from where you were (culture of origin) into your new environment (culture of competition) you are likely to encounter losses of relationships, security, and confidence. The inability to let go of outgrown or unhealthy attachments can lead to unhealthy behaviors and emotional states that will hinder your personal and professional growth.

INSIGHTS AND STRATEGIES

1. Acknowledge the impact of relationships that are changing or that have been lost, and find safe outlets to express your feelings.
2. Appreciate the value of what you have lost. For example, detail the role a particular relationship played in your life during a certain period of times that is now past.
3. Accept that losses are a difficult part of the journey and are necessary for continued growth.
4. Accommodate the emotional (internal and external) backlash. In other words, be patient with yourself and others.
5. Adjust to the new realities while staying open to new discoveries and relationships.
6. Always remember that acceptance is not a weakness. It is a skill when employed appropriately, and from a psychological standpoint, it frees you up to concentrate on where you can make your greatest impact.

AFTERWORD

I want to end this book by again congratulating you on your accomplishments. It is easy to get lost in the chaos and lose sight of the importance of what you have achieved thus far. Your hard work has gotten you this far, and my mission is to help you maximize your opportunities and to create opportunities for others—my definition of true success. I'll be the first to tell you that surviving success is impossible to do without support. To a certain degree, we all learn the hard way. But at the same time we can lessen the heartache of others having to discover these truths for themselves. My hope is that the critical skills described in this book are a compass for you as you navigate the treacherous seas of high achievement.

In addition to the skills you need in order to sustain the success you have achieved thus far, it is important to remember that you are not alone. It is okay to ask for help. Instead of viewing it as a weakness, think of getting support as your competitive advantage. In our complex, competitive society, those with the slightest edge often win. The point, of course, is to win without losing who you are. In order for that to happen we need the skills presented in this book—and we also need to recognize that these skills are ingredients which can be incorporated into the larger concept of resilience.

As we have discussed throughout our work together, there

may be variables that accompany high achievement or success, many of which are unintended or unexpected. It is impossible to prepare for everything that will come your way but there are ways to position yourself to be better able to handle things when they come. Understanding the concept of resilience is helpful toward this end. Resilience can be defined as the ability to bounce back from adversity or the ability to adapt positively in adverse conditions.

In order to thrive in a high-achievement environment you have to raise your level of resilience. You will make mistakes and wrong turns. That is only natural when you are dealing in the unknown. Yet, if there is one thing I know, it is that we are more resilient than we give ourselves credit for.

And so, how do we recognize our resilience and continue to develop it? The secret to thriving in the limelight comes down to three words: strategy, structure, and support. In fact, the summation of all of the skills presented in this book can be encompassed into these three tasks. Although they may sound like they are common sense, we know that common sense is not always common practice.

Develop a strategy: The key to dealing with the inevitable challenges that accompany success is to first anticipate that there will be potential pitfalls and consider what they may be. You won't be familiar with all that will come your way so that is why it is important to do your research. Ask those knowledgeable in the area of success what to expect. If you are already on the steep upward curve of high achievement take the time to identify where most of your frustrations stem from. With this knowledge you can start to build a strategy that is designed to alleviate the major avenues of stress. The psychological advantage of developing a strategy is that it gives you a greater sense of control and confidence, which enables a greater degree of flexibility when it comes to challenges. The strategy doesn't have to be perfect. It just needs to be in place and adjusted accordingly as you go on.

Build a structure: As we saw earlier in the book, systems and routines help keep you aligned with your highest priorities. Whether it is earmarking time weekly to spend with your family and friends, or taking time to consistently study and read journals about your field of interest, developing good habits early will help keep you focused and effective. Once you have a good weekly or monthly system, stick with it when things get crazy—that's what it is there for, to help provide stability when things feel like they are out of hand.

Seek out support: Asking for help can be difficult but not asking for it can be devastating. Connect with colleagues, mentors, coaches, or consultants as a way of gaining perspectives that will lead to the necessary growth for sustained success. Although tempting, resist the urge to go at it alone even if this is what you have always done. Remaining open and coachable, knowing that there is strength in vulnerability, will greatly fortify your resilience. As one of my clients who suffered a massive fall from grace said upon getting therapeutic help, "My hope is that if I can learn to trust you, then perhaps someday I can learn to trust and eventually love myself." Indeed, healthy support can make all the difference.

ONE MORE THING ...

I want to relay a message that has served me well in my years of service. It is a story about a highly successful pastor of a large community. He was recognized not only locally but nationally for the positive impact he was making in the community. However, this successful pastor became depressed and started to withdraw. His depression had gotten to the point where he was contemplating taking his own life. As he was making the preparations he decided to get on his knees and pray one last time. With tears running down his face, he asked God why he felt so bad. "I have built up a great church that is saving many souls. I have built housing facilities for the poor. I go visit the hospitals to give hope to the sick. I am on many boards that help the community. I have done all of this and received so much in return that I need for nothing, so why do I feel so hopeless and dismayed?" As he sat there in silence, he received his answer in a still soft voice. "You have truly been faithful, but you made one big mistake. You have given so much that your cup is empty, but yet you try to continue to operate from it . You feel this way because you never took the time to fill your own cup. So, what you need to do now is get off your knees, get back into the world, and focus on filling your cup. So that now when you serve, you will be operating from the overflow."

My challenge to you is that, amidst the intense challenges of surviving success, you take back the reins of your life by becoming more present and intentional. As you shine you will inevitably ignite the fire in others. So, go out and fill your cup, and operate from the overflow.

—Dr. Tim Benson

ABOUT THE AUTHOR

Dr. Timothy Gerard Benson is an Instructor in Psychiatry, Part-time at Harvard Medical School and founder of Gamewise Consulting LLC, a company that provides strategic support for elite performers and their families. Often referred to as "The Success Psychiatrist," Dr. Benson's motto is "Helping the Best Get Better." With a decade of experience as a clinical instructor at Harvard Medical School, he has helped professional athletes, entertainers and executives manage the unintended consequences of their achievements, while simultaneously helping them better their best.

A native of Jefferson City, Missouri and a three sport high school athlete, Dr. Benson attended Hampton University on a full football scholarship. He was the recipient of multiple national scholar athlete awards including National Leader of the Year by Toyota/Black Entertainment Television (BET) and was one of 12 recipients of the National Football Foundation and College Hall of Fame Scholar Athlete Award in 1993. Upon graduation he was awarded Hampton University's highest honor—The President's Cup.

He completed his medical degree at the University of Rochester School of Medicine and adult psychiatry residency at Harvard Medical School's Massachusetts General Hospital/McLean Hospital where he served as a chief resident in his final year. As an addiction psychiatrist he became the

Medical Director at both The McLean Center at Fernside and The McLean Residence at the Brook, two nationally acclaimed residential addiction facilities.

He has also served as a treating clinician in the NBA/NBPA Player Assistance/Anti-Drug Program.

In addition to his clinical work and coaching programs for athletes, entertainers and entrepreneurs, Dr. Benson speaks nationally on the topics of "Outperforming Yourself", "Succeeding Against the Odds" and "Surviving Success". He has also been an invited panelist at Harvard Business School and Wharton School of Business to address the psychological dynamics of being the "first in the family" to reach certain social, economic and educational milestones.

To contact Dr. Benson about media appearances, speaking to your team, staff, or at your next event, visit: www.drtimothybenson.com.

To connect with Dr. Benson on Twitter, follow: @drtimbenson.

CPSIA information can be obtained at www.ICGtesting.com
Printed in the USA
BVOW06s0219100816

458532BV00013B/67/P

9 780990 898405